# The Eleventh Commandment

# The Eleventh Commandment

## Caring for Creation:
## Words of Wisdom from the
## World's Great Faith Traditions

Edited by

## Christine Williams

Earth Faith Publications

Earth Faith Publications
www.earthfaith.net

14  13  12  11  10    5  4  3  2  1

**Library of Congress Cataloging-in-Publication Data**

The eleventh commandment : caring for creation : words of wisdom from the
world's great faith traditions / edited by Christine Williams; foreword by Bill
McKibben.

Cover Design: David Sheets

p. cm.

Includes bibliographical references and index.

ISBN 1456307371 (trade paper : alk. paper)

1. Nature—Religious aspects—Christianity. 2. Human ecology—Religious
aspects—Christianity. 3. Nature—Religious aspects. 4. Human ecology—
Religious aspects. I. Williams, Christine, 1957-

BT695.5.E575 2011 201'.77—dc22

# Contents

# Contributors

**Dr. John B. Cobb, Jr.**—Professor Emeritus at the Claremont Graduate University and the Claremont School of Theology, and co-founder of the Center for Process Studies

**The Reverend Dr. Janet L. Parker**—Winner of the first annual Environmental Sermon Contest, sponsored by the National Council of Churches

**The Most Reverend Dr. Katharine Jefferts Schori**—The Presiding Bishop of the Episcopal Church

**The Very Reverend Dr. Samuel T. Lloyd III**—Dean of the Washington National Cathedral

**Rabbi Arthur Waskow**—Director of The Shalom Center

**Dr. Shahid Athar, M.D.**—Clinical Associate Professor at Indiana University School of Medicine, and Past President of The Islamic Medical Association of North America

**Dr. Matthew Sleeth, M.D.**—Author of "Serve God, Save the Planet" and "The Gospel According to the Earth"

**Nancy Sleeth**—Author of "Go Green, Save Green"

**Reverend Alida DeCoster**—Minister to the Social Justice Internship Program at The Unitarian Universalist Washington DC Office

*Contributors*

**Rabbi Stephen S. Pearce**—Rabbi of The Congregation Emanu-El in San Francisco, and author

**Dr. Muzammil H. Siddiqi**—Past president of the Islamic Society of North America (two terms), and Professor of Religious Studies at Chapman University

**Most Reverend Harry J. Flynn, D.D.**—Archbishop Emeritus of Saint Paul and Minneapolis, Minnesota

**Dr. Tony Campolo**—Founder of the Evangelical Association for the Promotion of Education, author, and media commentator

**The Reverend Canon Sally Grover Bingham**—Priest, and founder and president of The Interfaith Power and Light Campaign

**Dr. Zayn Kassam**—Professor of Religion at Pomona College

**Rabbi Warren Stone**—Rabbi of Temple Emanuel in the greater metropolitan area of Washington D.C.

**Dr. Ignacio Castuera**—Methodist minister, National Chaplain for Planned Parenthood, and editor of a book of sermons

**Dr. Safei Hamed**—Professor and Director of the Landscape Architecture Programs at Chatham University in Pittsburgh, Pennsylvania, and expert on Islam and the environment

**The Reverend Dr. Bob Edgar**—President of Common Cause, and six-term member of the U.S. House of Representatives

# Acknowledgements

It is here that I offer my heartfelt gratitude to everyone who helped in the creation of this project. I would like to thank Dr. David M. Standlea, author of *Oil, Globalization, and the War for the Arctic Refuge*, for teaching me about environmental issues and climate change, and for recommending outstanding books for me to read. I credit my pastor, Dr. Ignacio Castuera, with indirectly giving me the idea for this book. (Dr. Castuera edited a book of sermons in 1992 entitled *Dreams on Fire: Embers of Hope: From the Pulpits of Los Angeles After the Riots.*) I would also like to thank Dr. Castuera for contributing a sermon to this project, and for introducing me to Dr. John B. Cobb, Jr., whose superb essay, "Hope on a Dying Planet," became the first chapter of this book. I will be eternally grateful to Dr. Cobb, who was gracious enough to offer advice on many occasions, and to allow me to post sections of my August 2010 interview with him on YouTube.

I would like to thank The Reverend Canon Sally G. Bingham for her sermon, and for her help in connecting me with other religious leaders. Chloe Schwabe, former National Council of Churches Eco-Justice Specialist, also very generously helped me find contributors to the project, including The Reverend Dr. Janet Parker, winner of the first annual Environmental Sermon Contest sponsored by the National Council of Churches.

Matthew and Nancy Sleeth were very kind to share excerpts from their published works. Will Sears, former Director of Communication for the Sleeths' organization Blessed Earth, was helpful in facilitating permission for the Sleeths' contribution to this book. Tyler Edgar worked tirelessly to deliver the Reverend Dr. Bob Edgar's sermon. James Warren helped me obtain permission from Basic Books for the use of a remarkable chapter from Dr. Tony Campolo's book *Letters to a Young Evangelical*.

My friend, Dr. Zayn Kassam, offered advice, encouragement, and editorial support as the project progressed, and has contributed a thought provoking essay to the manuscript. David Sheets designed a beautiful cover for the book using his own photography. A charming and informative website for the book (www.earthfaith.net) was created by Crystal Yachin Lee. Bill Scott (D. & F. Scott Publishing, Inc.) completed 90% of the work required to turn this manuscript into a book, but unfortunately was unable to finish the project due to ALS. If you ever need tech support, I hope you are fortunate enough to find talented people like Jack Shih and Ryan Sheh. I received steadfast support from John Meisner, and from my sister, Dr. Nancy A. Williams, without whose encouragement this book would more than likely have remained an unfulfilled dream.

And of course, I will be forever indebted to all of the religious leaders and writers who generously chose to contribute a sermon or essay to this project. There would be no book without them.

# Foreword

## *Bill McKibben*

Ten years ago it was exceptionally rare to find a sermon, or a book of theology, that reflected on the environment. Ten years hence, it's the absence of such comment that will be considered odd. As this stalwart collection makes clear, we've passed a tipping point, and faith communities are finally beginning to understand the importance of the environment. Beginning to understand the importance of their actions for the world, but at least as important, beginning to understand the importance of these reflections for the church, the synagogue, the mosque.

It's no wonder that we were slow to take these questions up in church. For most of human history, it's been the relationship between people and other people, or sometimes between people and God, that's been fraught—that needed attention. But in recent years that's begun to change, and change fast. In short order, we've grown so large as a species—in numbers but especially in appetites—that we're now threatening to overwhelm the very systems we've taken for granted. The damage we're doing can only be described as biblical: if you've visited New Orleans recently, you suddenly understand Noah.

And in a society where political life is dominated by a fixation on More—on endless economic growth, even past the point of satiation—only religious communities have some hope of fixing that broken relationship. Mosques and synagogues and churches are our last institutions that can remember some goal other than accumulation for human existence.

But religion needs environmentalism as badly as environmentalism needs religion. For if we allow ourselves to de-create the planet we've been given, we'll soon find that our faiths make far less sense. I'm a Methodist; I know that if you took all the hymns out of our hymnal that described the glory of God through the actions of nature, you'd have a book half as thick (and with most of the good songs gone). To the religious mind, the earth is a museum of divine intent, and desecrating that museum is as sad an act of looting as one can imagine.

It's been thrilling in recent years to see how creative pastors and rabbis and imams and laypeople have become as they confront the environmental crisis. Interfaith Power and Light; What Would Jesus Drive?; the Evangelical Statement on Climate Change; Shomrei Adamah; the Evangelical Environmental Network; Quaker Earthcare Witness; Earth Ministry; Religious Witness for the Environment; the Au Sable Institute; the Unitarian Seventh Principle Movement; and a hundred more initiatives in every corner of the country make it clear that the environment will in the future be as important as war and peace, poverty, and moral issues on the religious agenda. And that, too, it may be the one issue that most easily unites us all.

# Introduction

This book is a labor of love for my children. The 20th century environmentalist David Brower wisely observed, "We do not inherit the Earth from our fathers, we are borrowing it from our children." After learning that a variety of factors are changing this planet's climate and placing our children's future at great risk, I could not remain silent. As a life-long Methodist, I had hoped that Christians would be sounding the alarm and calling people of faith to care for this beautiful planet with which God has entrusted us. To my dismay, I did not hear much emphasis being placed on living more sustainably when I first began work on this project, at least within my local community of faith.

Over the course of the past few years, I found it incredibly heartening to connect with so many people of faith across the United States who care deeply about the earth. When I began this journey, I received many letters from both local and nationally known ministers and professors who were enthusiastic about my project, but who did not have a sermon or essay about faith and the environment to contribute. Still, these letters spurred me on. If well-respected religious leaders found merit in my project, I might be on to something.

My goal all along has been to find a way to get the word out to as many people as possible that caring for creation is a moral and ethical issue that we can no longer afford to ignore.

We must break away from the unlimited-growth paradigm and begin to live our lives in simpler ways. My hope is that readers of this book will be inspired and informed, leading to lifestyle changes that, en masse, will have profound repercussions on the rest of the world. There is no doubt that we (as Americans) are living in a culture of consumerism which tends to lead us away from matters of the spirit.

Since I am a Christian, I initially intended for this book to be an appeal to other Christians to join the fight to save the planet. However, after hearing Bruce Feiler interviewed on the radio show *Speaking of Faith* about his book, *Abraham: A Journey to the Heart of Three Faiths*, I knew without a doubt that this book needed to take an interfaith approach. I am excited about the opportunity for this book to open a window of understanding between the monotheistic faiths. The interfaith approach also speaks to the necessity to unite in our efforts "to save this fragile earth," to borrow a title from the sermon of The Very Reverend Dr. Samuel T. Lloyd III (Chapter 4).

The climate crisis is a very complex dilemma involving many interrelated factors. I want the reader to understand first of all the call to care for creation that is in each of our respective scriptures; secondly, to understand how high levels of consumption, affluence, finite resources, and over-population, etc., combine to lead us to the brink of catastrophe; and lastly, to be offered practical suggestions about what we can do as people of faith to live more sustainably.

For hundreds of years, you could hear church bells ringing to gather people together for important announcements. We need to ring the bells, and sound the shofar, and listen to the Muslim call for prayer until all people who gather together in the name of their God look upward and outward and are so struck by the beauty of the heavens and the earth that their hearts and minds are transformed. I have a vision of people of all faiths coming together, willing to sacrifice and to be steadfast stewards of the earth, to ensure a livable planet, not just for themselves, but for many generations to come. In the words of former Supreme Court Justice William O. Douglas:

> When the Earth, its products, it creatures become his concern, man is caught up in a cause greater than his own life and more meaningful. Only when man loses himself in an endeavor of that magnitude does he walk and live with humility and reverence.

Please join me in this journey of discovering what your God calls you to do in caring for creation. If your journey is anything like mine, you will not only find yourself seeing God's creation through new eyes, but also walking in closer communion and deeper relationship with our Creator. In the words of Ralph Waldo Emerson, "Nature is the art of God."

Christine Williams
Claremont, California
February 2011

# —1—
# *Hope on a Dying Planet*

## *Dr. John B. Cobb, Jr.*

*Dr. John B. Cobb, Jr. was born in Japan in 1925 to parents who were Methodist missionaries. He has become a prominent theologian who is possibly best known for the crucial role he played in the development of process theology. He is the author of many groundbreaking books and articles. He is professor emeritus at the Claremont Graduate University and the Claremont School of Theology. This essay was written in 1970 and recently updated. Dr. Cobb's message is clearly still as compelling and relevant as it was when it was originally written.*

The universe is mostly a vast, almost empty, expanse of space-time. Scattered through it in an uneven, but not quite random way are innumerable stars. Around some of these revolve satellites we call planets. One of these planets revolving around a star of modest size is alive. We call that planet Earth.

Perhaps there are other living planets circling other stars in this or other galaxies. Perhaps in whatever universe there was before the "Big Bang" that gave birth to this one, there were other living beings. We do not know. But indications are that the other planets in this solar system are lifeless. In an area to be measured in light years, if not in all the infinities of time and space, we are alone.

This planet has not always been alive. Indeed, as Richard Overman has reminded us, if we conceive the five billion years of the Earth's past as though recorded in ten volumes of five hundred pages each, so that each page records a million years, cellular life appears only in the eighth volume, about a billion years ago. The story of all the plants and animals of the Cambrian era occupies only the tenth volume, and of this the first half is taken up with how plants became terrestrial and the amphibians emerged. Around page 440 of this 500-page book the reptiles reach the height of their development. It is not until page 465 that their dominance is superseded by that of birds and warm-blooded animals.

Finally, on page 499 of this tenth volume man appears. The last two words on the last page recount his story from the rise of civilization six thousand years ago until the present.

Throughout the last two volumes, life proliferated itself, creating an environment in which more complex forms of life could emerge and prosper. Both life and the capacity to support life increased millennia after millennia. Man entered the scene in a planet that was biologically very rich indeed. To that organic richness he contributed little. Indeed, in certain localities over limited periods of time, his treatment of his environment was quite destructive. But only when we reach the last letter of the last word on the last page does he turn the tide against life. Only then does man begin the process of killing the planet. What is astonishing is that all that has been produced over a billion years is so vulnerable to destruction by the latecomer to the scene.

Yet it should not surprise us that what takes so long to create can be so easily destroyed. It took only a moment for an assassin's bullet to destroy the complex richness of the life of a John F. Kennedy or a Martin Luther King, Jr. That richness of thought, will, and feeling had been many years in the making, but it depended on an organic base that could be destroyed almost instantaneously. The life of the planet similarly depends on a physical base which, now that its secrets have been mastered by man, is vulnerable to his destruction. For at least a hundred years and with accelerating acceleration, we are now destroying it. The eleventh volume may recount the much poorer story of a lifeless planet.

This perspective on ourselves is important because of the profound illusions we Westerners, and especially we Americans, have entertained about our natural environment. We have supposed, consciously or unconsciously, that it is inexhaustible and indestructible. Of course, we have known that a few species of wildlife were becoming extinct and that here and there we had turned fertile fields into dust-bowls, but these were felt as isolated phenomena having nothing to do with our basic situation. We thought that we could learn lessons from our mistakes and through ever-increasing scientific knowledge and technological skill advance to new heights of prosperity and happiness. We might worry about the loss of some prized moral and spiritual values, but our pictures of future life were always in terms of fantastic progress in science and technology, comfort and prosperity. In this scenario, Nature was cast in the role of supplier of limitless resources for our use and enjoyment.

I have begun to realize how fully I have myself lived out of these basic assumptions. I used to wonder idly where all the smoke and fumes went that our industrial society belches into the air, but until I came to California I was satisfied with the answer that the wind blew it away. I used to wonder idly where all the waste and sewage went that our hygienic culture so quickly makes invisible, but until I saw Lake Erie, I was satisfied with the answer that it was carried out to sea. Atmosphere and ocean seemed inexhaustible in their size. And in relation to the technology and industry of a hundred years ago, although theoretically false, this may have been practically true. But no more. The wedding of science and technology in the past century has given man the power to transform the environment radically, not merely locally, but globally. Today it is not the atmosphere over cities alone, but the planetary atmosphere that is polluted. Los Angeles smog contaminates the air of Yellowstone, and the filth that is breathed in Tokyo is blown across the Pacific Ocean to be added to the vast local pollution in California. The continental shelf near the United States and the coral reefs and islands of the South Seas are already threatened with extinction.

## An Alternative to Complacency

Although in some respects our past actions have begun irreversible processes that must now run their destructive course, for the most part, we could prevent the further dying of the planet. We could call a halt to the poisoning of air and water, for example. But this would require the most drastic alteration of our economy. We would have to greatly reduce the gross national product, whose annual increase has been the aim of every administration and the supposed measure of our national health. It would require new types of communities far less dependent than ours on motor transportation and industrial products in general. It would require drastic alteration of our individual goals, an orientation of our lives around their contribution to the life and future of the planet rather than ourselves, our families, our nations, or even humanity.

Even this drastic and unforeseeable change of our total style of life will be insufficient if population cannot be adequately fed without the use of ecologically destructive chemicals in fertilizers and insecticides. Continued population growth could not but accelerate the process of killing the planet in its desperate efforts to eke out a living from what is left of water and soil. The survival of human beings is bound up with the necessity of stabilizing and even reducing our population.

Some of you will justifiably be thinking that my language is exaggerated. The poisoning of air and water, even when their probable side effects are taken into consideration, probably will not destroy all life. The inability of the planet to support its present human population does not mean that humans will necessarily become extinct, but only that in one way or another population will be drastically cut back—perhaps by famine, perhaps by pestilence, perhaps by war.

The problem is complicated, however, by the fact that humans do have at their disposal weapons capable of exterminating the human race along with man's animal cousins. Since Hiroshima and Nagasaki, we have lived under the threat of a new kind of war. Thus far the balance of terror has worked, and the bombs have not been used again. We survived the Cuban confrontation, and we may survive the confrontation with the Middle East.

But can we really expect that the balance of terror will forever restrain the use of atomic weapons as they spread into more and more hands? Will nations facing genocidal annihilation or wholesale starvation restrain themselves so that others may survive?

How do we react to this somber picture of our situation? Let me speak for myself while you formulate your own answer. My first and most common reaction is refusal of serious belief. The individual facts I may not be able to dispute, but I deny to myself that the situation is really that bad. The authorities with all the power and knowledge at their disposal will certainly take care of it. I should put in my two cents worth on this issue as on others to salve my conscience and to bolster my self-image as a concerned citizen, but beyond that, I shall conduct business as usual, assuming that the future will be much like the past, putting out of my mind the truly apocalyptic threat under which we live.

However, there are times when the recognition of the planet's dying breaks through my defenses. Then my reaction tends to be one of despair. If present trends lead toward the lessening of the quality of human life, must we not realistically accept the lessened quality of human life as inevitable? What use is it to attempt the impossible task of altering the course of history, especially when my influence is so slight?

It is important to recognize the great similarity of these two responses of complacency and despair. Their results are almost identical. They let me off the hook. I am left free to eat, drink, and be merry—or more realistically, to enjoy my family, my friends, and my work—for there is no real problem to whose solution I am called to contribute. Either others will solve it or it is insoluble. My attention can be directed toward the more immediate and manageable issues of daily living.

My title is "Hope on a Dying Planet." Realistic hope represents a third alternative to complacency and despair. The person who hopes can view the threat unflinchingly. He does not deny its seriousness either in his thoughts or in his feelings. Yet his hope is the refusal of despair. The one who hopes is the one who seeks openings, assumes responsibility, endures failure after failure, and still seeks new openings for fresh efforts.

In the depths of a depression, Franklin Delano Roosevelt once said that the only thing we had to fear was fear itself. Today, we might say analogously, our only hope is hope itself. If we react in complacency or despair, there is no hope for human survival. If, instead, we hope, the future lies before us, full of uncertainties and desperate risks, yet containing also hope.

But how can there be hope? To tell ourselves to hope in order that there be hope is, in the long run, futile. Hope rests on something other than its own usefulness. A partial answer is that hope is a matter of temperament or disposition, something to be dealt with, if at all, by psychologists. Perhaps such a temperament is closely connected with the basic trust one develops in early months of life when one is fortunate in having quality parental care.

But there are other grounds of hope, grounds we can call existential, or religious, or even theological. In some measure, hope is a function of what we believe, and in this cosmic and global crisis, it is most clearly a function of what we believe ultimately and comprehensively.

In Psalm 33:22 it is written, "Let thy steadfast love, O Lord, be upon us, according as we hope in Thee." The Psalmist speaking in this text is clear that our hope is in the Lord and his mercy. He found none in the analysis of historical trends. His picture of the Lord is anthropomorphic—rather crudely so for our taste. He is viewed as an omnipotent figure standing outside the processes of nature and history and controlling them so as to help those who hope in his mercy.

Few of us can live out that vision of reality, and its collapse in the last three centuries seems to have removed the grounds of hope for many people. In much of our youth culture, hope is focused on short-term goals and easily shattered when these are not realized. The quest for kicks, or mystical meaning or celebration of life in the present moment, is in part an expression of the loss of hope, a loss we older people have bequeathed to our children. Is there, nevertheless, for us a ground of hope somehow equivalent to that of the Psalmist?

## Our Hope is in More Than Hope Itself

I cannot speak for all people, or for all religious people, or even for all Christians. But for myself the answer is "yes." The fact that, when chemical conditions make it possible, life appears, with growth and reproduction, means to me that there is that in reality that calls life forth and forward and strives against the forces of inertia and death. The fact that the human psyche is capable of being claimed by truth and touched by concern for fellow human beings means to me that there is that in reality that calls forth honesty and love and strives against the retreat into security, narrow interests, and merely habitual behavior. This power works slowly and quietly, by persuasion, not calling attention to itself. It does not present itself for observation by biologist or psychologist, yet it is presupposed in both the organism he studies and in his own faithful pursuit of truth. It is not to be found somewhere outside the organisms in which it is at work, but it is not to be identified with them either. We can conceive it best as Spirit.

For me it is the belief in this Spirit, the giver of life and love, that is the ground of hope. In spite of all the destructive forces man lets loose against life on this planet, the Spirit of Life is at work in ever new and unforeseeable ways, countering and circumventing the obstacles humans put in its path. In spite of my strong tendencies to complacency and despair, I experience the Spirit in myself as calling forth the realistic hope apart from which there is no hope, and I am confident that what I find in myself is occurring in you as well.

Because I believe that what makes for life and love and hope is not simply my decision or yours, but a Spirit that moves us both, I do not have to suppose that my own efforts are of great consequence in order to believe them to be worthwhile. I can recognize that they may even be futile or misdirected and still persist in them as long as no clearer light is given. For I see what I do as part of something much greater, in which each of you participates also, to whatever extent each sensitively responds to the insights and opportunities that come your way. Belief in the Spirit is belief that I am not alone; that in working for life and love in hope I am working with something much greater than myself; that there are possibilities for the future that cannot be simply projected out of the past; that even my mistakes and failures may be woven into a healing pattern of which I cannot now form any conception.

The openness of the future, the occurrence of the unpredictable, the surprising fruition of forgotten seeds, have been illustrated for me in regard to the ecology/population crisis. I myself have been aware of its seriousness since the summer of 1969. At that time, one who was concerned felt like a voice crying in the wilderness. No popular national magazine had taken up the issue. The church seemed silent. Politicians avoided the question. Only a few weary ecologists, nature lovers, and demographers kept up the apparently fruitless struggle to alert the nation before it was too late. The very word, "ecology," was hardly known.

Over the years, much has changed. The news media has taken it up. New organizations have arisen and others gained fresh vitality. Politicians are now vying with each other to show their concern. Climatologists are in great demand. Global warming has become a household phrase.

Economists and ecologists still speak at cross-purposes, and we must listen to both. This issue is tied up with every other issue, and any step we take toward its solution has ramifications in other areas that are often bitter indeed. Based on past experience, the prospect of sustained effort on the part of the masses of men and women is poor. But the future need not repeat the past. That depends on us, on our ability to maintain a realistic hope. If we refuse to be distracted, face the difficulties, recognize the complex interrelations of all our problems, and endure, there is reason for hope.

## The Spirit of Life and Love and Hope

The situation has been pictured as if the world were a ship on a long voyage. The ship has first class and steerage. The crew direct their attention to the comforts of the first class passengers, who have plenty of space, luxurious accommodations, and superabundant food of great delicacy and richness. In steerage, men and women are crowded and uncomfortable. The food is tasteless and poorly cooked. Some suffer from malnutrition. Contagious diseases break out, and medical help is inadequate. Tempers are high, and fights occur. First class passengers occasionally look down on the steerage deck below with amusement and even with pity, but for the most part they prefer to forget the existence of these other passengers and enjoy the gracious living for which they have paid, along with their cultivated companions. The fact that most of the steerage passengers are of different cultures and races makes this easier.

Many of the steerage passengers dream of someday transferring to first class, and a few even succeed in doing so. But most resign themselves to the impossibility of such a move. They live in impotent envy, taking out their anger on each other. However, a few among them begin whispering that this is unnecessary. Why should they be crowded and poorly fed when there is so much space and food wasted on the other decks? Why not share all the space and food equally?

Many pooh-pooh the idea as impossible, but others listen. Of these, some want to seize by force the space and food they need, while others propose appealing to the innate sense of fair play on the part of the first class passengers. At first these win out, and a few changes result from their humble and modest requests. The food supply and medical attention are improved. The first class passengers expect gratitude, but in fact the slight success only intensifies the demands for an equal share.

I will not detail the struggle as it grows bloody and bitter. The crew is called in by the first class passengers to maintain order and guarantee their privileges—for which, after all, they have paid. And the crew obliges with all too little reluctance. The few first class passengers who sympathize with the steerage passengers are increasingly ostracized. More important, many of the children of the first class passengers believe in the cause of the steerage passengers and try to help them.

Several times during the struggle the news is heard that the boat has sprung a leak. A few members of the crew are dispatched to see about it. They report that it is not too large a leak yet, although it is growing. Most suppose the captain will see to it, and they go about their business and pleasure. But the captain is too busy trying to keep order, and the few who keep inquiring about the leak are ignored.

The untended leak becomes larger. Some of the ship's supplies are soaked in salt water and ruined. Even the boat's speed is slightly affected. New leaks begin to appear. Although life continues luxurious in first class, some notice that the ship lists a little. Some of the shipboard games are adversely affected. Shuffleboard is abandoned. More voices are raised about the urgency of action, but when the crew shoot some of the children, a new controversy breaks out which distracts attention.

The first class passengers feel guilty about the killing of these children, but they cannot bring themselves to admit that they are in the wrong. They devote their energies to self-justification. The children are deeply hurt by this attitude of their parents. Until now they have felt that the ideals on which they have acted were those of their parents as well, and that if only the parents saw the situation clearly they would aid the steerage passengers instead of using force against them. With far less confidence, the steerage passengers have shared this hope. But the willingness of the parents to kill their own children in order to maintain their privileges and their subsequent justification of this act are profoundly disillusioning. A few turn to unalloyed violence. Most relapse into angry but lethargic resignation.

The ship continues to list. Almost everyone recognizes it now. But in the aftermath of the intense emotions generated by the other conflicts, no one seems to care very much. Leaders vie with each other to announce their concern, but none dares speak realistically of the risk or of the vast cost of dealing with it. The people have no stomach for great sacrifice. Their idealism is spent.

This is where we are now. What happens next is still unsettled. We may continue to fragment into disgruntled and frustrated minorities while the frantic efforts of our leaders to hold us together leave little energy to deal with the spreading leaks. Only when the water covers the lower decks will the passengers turn their attention too late to the problems of a sinking ship. With bitter mutual recriminations they will struggle for places in the inadequate lifeboats, while the sinking ship carries most to their deaths.

Another possibility is that the crew and first class passengers somehow wall off part of the ship in such a way that when the lower decks are filled with water, the steerage passengers drown and most of the supplies are lost, but many of the first class passengers can survive, although at a level of subsistence inferior to that of the steerage passengers when the boat was intact.

A third possibility is that the ship's captain, as a man of wisdom and courage, will persuade all the passengers of the necessity of immediate massive action. Unnecessary supplies are then quickly thrown overboard, including many of the weapons used by the crew to control the steerage passengers. All able-bodied men join together in a massive effort to pump out the water and repair the leaks. In the process, the mutual antagonisms subside. New leadership patterns are established. All the passengers and the crew as well become a single community living frugally but harmoniously together.

Granted, only a miracle could realize this third possibility. Politicians would have to refrain from playing upon the mutual antagonisms of our polarized society and challenge us to extremely unpopular sacrifices. And masses of people would have to vote for and follow these politicians. Business and industry would have to adopt entirely new criteria by which to measure achievements, and all of us, dependent on the present system for our luxuries, would have to accept a far simpler style of life. Is all that really possible? To believe it is, is to believe even beyond all evidence in the power of the Spirit of Life and Love and Hope.

Belief in the Spirit is no grounds for complacency. There is no guarantee that people will respond to the Spirit's promptings in sufficient numbers and with sufficient sensitivity to begin the healing of the planet. But there is the possibility. The future can be different from the past. Therefore, there is hope. While there is life, there *is* hope.

The Psalmist spoke of hope in the Lord. I have spoken of hope in the Spirit. There is no conflict. The Lord is the Spirit. What is of utmost importance is that each of us grounds our life in the basis for realistic hope and that we attend to that in reality which makes for life and love.

# —2—

# *From Apocalypse to Genesis*

## *The Reverend Dr. Janet L. Parker*

*The Reverend Dr. Janet L. Parker is an ordained United Church of Christ minister who is currently pastor for Parish Life at Rock Spring Congregational United Church of Christ in Arlington, Virginia. Dr. Parker graduated with her Master of Divinity from Princeton Theological Seminary, and received her Ph.D. in Christian Ethics at Union Theological Seminary in New York with a focus on ecological and economic ethics. Her thesis focused on ecofeminist and indigenous perspectives on sustainable development. Following the September 11th attacks, Dr. Parker served the Presbytery of New York as coordinator of disaster relief. From 2002 to 2004, she taught Christian Ethics at Chicago Theological Seminary. The following year, she worked on a postdoctoral fellowship at Princeton University's Center for the Study of Religion. For the past several years, Dr. Parker has served on a theological advisory team accompanying the World Council of Churches' Decade to Overcome Violence initiative. She is the author of numerous articles, and a chapter in the book* Global Neighbors: Christian Faith and Moral Obligation in Today's Economy *(Eerdmans 2008). The following sermon by Dr. Parker won the top prize in the first annual Environmental Sermon Contest sponsored by the National Council of Churches in 2007.*

Ezekiel 36:22, 24–36
John 3:1–10
Revelation 22:1–5

Today's service is in honor of Earth Day, and yesterday, the Rock Spring community came together in an extraordinary way to celebrate the goodness of God's creation and to highlight our role as stewards of creation in our first-ever Earth Day festival.

The Earth Day festival was a symphony of creative and inspiring activities that demonstrated our love for the Earth and various ways that we can care for creation and minimize our harmful impacts on the planet. Yet while the mood was celebratory and fun, close attention to the creative exhibits revealed some discordant notes. For example, one of the exhibits that generated interest was the "enviroscape," an ingenious model that demonstrated how different forms of pollution like pesticides, animal waste, construction materials, litter, agricultural runoff, and oily residue from cars get flushed into our local streams and rivers and run down into the Chesapeake Bay. Exhibits like this reminded us that Earth Day is more than a celebration of nature, though it is surely that. But Earth Day is also implicitly a recognition that something has gone wrong in our relationship with the natural world, something that needs fixing—something that we might describe in religious terms as a call to repentance, and even conversion.

Yet here we begin to tread on treacherous ground, because acknowledging the depth of the planetary crisis human beings have created is fraught with danger. I'm not speaking here of political danger, of the suppression of ecological truth by political leaders. I'm speaking of emotional and spiritual danger—the danger that recognition of the true magnitude of our ecological crisis will lead to paralysis and despair. If we are really paying attention, the drumbeat of news about ecological degradation and climate change not only evokes fear, but also a deep sadness. Because if we are tuned in, we sense on some level that the earth that we know and enjoy right now will not be the earth that our children and grandchildren inherit.

The signs are everywhere. Headlines scream at us: three-fourths of the rockfish in the Chesapeake Bay are diseased. The Shenandoah River is now listed as one of the top ten most endangered rivers in the nation. Glaciers and ice sheets in the Arctic and Antarctic are melting much faster than expected. Warming temperatures over the next century could turn agricultural land into desert, dry out the rain forests, raise sea levels, extinguish countless species, and cause disastrous storms. In fact, most scientists now say that climate change is not something facing us in the future, but is already here. The debate over whether global warming is happening is over. The only question is how bad will it get? Dr. Gustave Speth, Dean of the School of Forestry and Environmental Studies at Yale, was asked recently if environmental damage due to climate change could be prevented. "No," he replied. "It's too late for that. But we may still be able to prevent catastrophic damage." He concluded, "This is our last chance to get it right. We have run out of time."

Speth and many other scientists and theologians are speaking a language that sounds off-key to our modern ears. It's a language that biblical prophets like Ezekiel and John of Patmos would recognize, however. It is the language of apocalypse—the imagery of the end times and the mysteries of God. The environmental challenges that face us are beginning to look apocalyptic, except now the apocalypse is not a fantasy of fundamentalists, or the stuff of science fiction, but the edge of an abyss that clear-eyed scientists peer over and tremble at. And the threats we face are not orchestrated by God but self-inflicted.

It's hard to talk about these things, but we have to break the silence, especially within the churches, because here, above all else, we must speak the truth. As Daniel Maguire, a Catholic theologian, has said bluntly, "If current trends continue, we will not [survive] . . . If religion does not speak to [this], it is an obsolete distraction." And so we need to speak about it, and we need to weep about it, because it's only when we allow ourselves to actually feel what is going on that we will have the capacity to change it. As one ecofeminist theologian has said, "The capacity to weep and then do something is worth everything." This is the purpose of apocalyptic literature in the Bible and the purpose of the eco-apocalyptic warnings of scientists and environmentalists—not to paralyze us with fear, but to spur us to act, and even to invest us with hope.

Ezekiel, writing to exiles whose homeland had been destroyed, offered a vision of a new day—a dream of a time when they would return to their land and dwell in peace, when the land itself would be restored from its former desolation and bloom as if it were the garden of Eden. And the people who would dwell there would be different than the people who went into exile, because they would be transformed by their experience. They will return, but not as the same people, for we are told that God has cleansed them from their idols . . . and so, "a new heart I will give you, and a new spirit I will put within you; and I will remove from your body the heart of stone, and give you a heart of flesh." Isn't this what we so desperately need today? To have our hearts of stone removed, and in their place to receive hearts of flesh that can hear the crying of the earth? What we need, says Larry Rasmussen, is nothing less than conversion to the earth, because even our religion needs reformation. For too long, Christianity has been prone to earth-denying tendencies and nurtured fantasies of mastery and control over nature. The new reformation being called for means that "all religious and moral impulses of whatever sort must now be matters of unqualified earth-bound loyalty and care. Faith is fidelity to earth and full participation in its ecstasy and agony."

But the question remains, can Christianity be converted to the earth? Can Christianity become what Rasmussen calls "an earth faith"? It not only can, but it must. We search now for earth faith and earth ethics, because as Rasmussen explains, "society and nature together . . . is a community, without an exit. Whether we like it or not, it's life together now or not at all."

But there is good news. The good news is that we do have it within our faith to give us hope for the future and power to act and to change. The Bible itself is rich in resources, from its imagery of the Garden of Eden to the new Jerusalem—a new kind of garden—in the book of Revelation, which holds out a vision of a different way to live. In fact, some people say that apocalyptic literature is more about earth than it is about heaven. Because apocalyptic literature is written to people who are in crisis, who are struggling and desperate, people who need hope. Another meaning of the word "apocalypse" is revelation. Apocalypse reveals to us a new vision, not of heaven as pie in the sky but as heaven on earth. In fact, in the book of Revelation, heaven is not something we are raptured up to, but heaven is raptured down to us! Heaven is on earth, and God dwells on the new restored earth, as poisoned rivers become the river of the water of life. In apocalypse, sometimes we're taken through hell, but we return to Eden.

So today, I would like to suggest that we have to start reading the Bible backwards. That's our starting point. We begin with Revelation, not with the pristine garden. But then, reading backwards with the saints of all times and places, we discern the possibility for a new beginning—we reach towards a new genesis, a new way of living in harmony with the earth, a change of consciousness and a re-rooting of all of our religious traditions in eco-friendly soil. We have this capability to envision a new earth, and that was in abundant view yesterday when we saw the next generation at the Earth Day festival—most of the people there were under 20! They are going to be our teachers; they will lead us forward. And all of this is tied into what we're about to do, when we renew our baptismal vows in a few moments.

As we have this opportunity to touch the water—the water of life—which springs from the earth and is a gift from God—we have the chance to allow our consciousness to be transformed, to be converted to God and the earth. We have the opportunity to be born anew, not only as children of God but as children of the earth—as the new Adam and the new Eve who are committed to restoring creation, who are committed to serving the creation with nurturing love. And so as you come forward today, let this clean water wash away any indifference you have, any despair you feel, any fear that clouds your vision. And let it symbolize the outpouring of the Holy Spirit upon a transformed people. Let it remind us of the thirst of the earth and the thirst of the people in many parts of the world who live parched lives. Let it remind us of the dream of children to dance and bathe and drink clean water. Let it remind us of the promise of the scripture that streams will break forth in the desert, and that the river of the water of death will be replaced by the river of the water of life.

I would like to conclude with a poem by that great eco-poet Wendell Berry, who talks about how he deals with his despair and his fear and how he experiences grace:

> When Despair for the world grows within me
> and I wake in the night at the least sound
> in fear of what my life and my children's lives may be,
> I go and lie down where the wood drake
> rests in his beauty on the water, and the great heron feeds.
> I come into the peace of wild things
> who do not tax their lives with forethought
> of grief. I come into the presence of still water.
> And I feel above me the day-blind stars
> waiting with their light. For a time
> I rest in the grace of the world, and am free.

# —3—

# *Reflections on Poverty and Climate Change*

## *The Most Reverend Dr. Katharine Jefferts Schori*

*Katharine Jefferts Schori, D.D., Ph.D., is the Presiding Bishop of the Espiscopal Church in the United States. She is the first woman to be elected primate in the Anglican Communion. She earned a Bachelor of Science in Biology from Stanford University. She earned a Master of Science and a Ph.D. in Oceanography from Oregon State University. She earned her Master of Divinity in 1994 and was ordained as a priest that year. She was awarded a Doctor of Divinity in 2001 from The Church Divinity School of the Pacific. She is the author of three books. Her most recent book is* The Heartbeat of God: Finding the Sacred in the Middle of Everything *(Skylight Paths Pub, 2010).*

**The following essay was first published by the San Francisco Chronicle on May 20, 2007**

Before I became a priest, I was a professor of oceanography. One of the things I learned was that oceanographers couldn't just study squid or fish in isolation. We had to study interconnected systems. We had to understand not only the animals' environment, such as the water, but its chemistry and circulation, the atmosphere above the ocean and the geology below it. And that, I believe, is how we must understand our world: We must see everything, and everyone, as interconnected and intended by God to live in relationship.

Two of the most significant crises facing our world—climate change and deadly poverty—offer an example of such interconnectedness. By understanding how the two crises, and the people they affect, are connected, we can begin to understand how humanity can triumph over both. Extreme poverty—that is, poverty that kills— afflicts more than a billion of God's people around the world. Nearly 30,000 of these people will die today. That's 1 every three seconds. The factors that propel this kind of deadly poverty include hunger, diseases like AIDS and malaria, conflict, lack of access to education and basic inequality. Climate change threatens to make the picture even more deadly. As temperature changes increase the frequency and intensity of severe-weather events around the world, poor countries, which often lack infrastructural needs like storm walls and water-storage facilities, will divert previous resources away from fighting poverty in order to respond to disaster. Warmer climates will also increase the spread of diseases like malaria and tax the ability of poor countries to respond adequately. Perhaps most severely, changed rain patterns will increase the prevalence of drought in places like Africa, where only 4 percent of cropped land is irrigated, leaving populations without food and hamstrung in their ability to trade internationally to generate income.

Conversely, just as climate change will exacerbate poverty, poverty also is hastening climate change. Most poor people around the world lack access to a reliable-energy source, an imbalance that must be addressed in any attempt to lift a community out of poverty. Unfortunately, financial necessity often forces the choice of energy sources such as oil and coal that threaten to expand significantly the world's greenhouse emissions and thus accelerate the effects of climate change. This cycle—poverty that begets climate change, and vice versa—threatens the future of all people, rich and poor alike, and of all things in the world that God so loves.

This relationship between deadly poverty and the health of creation was not lost on the world's leaders when, at the turn of the twenty-first century, they committed to an ambitious yet attainable plan to cut global poverty in half by 2015. This plan, which established the eight Millennium Development Goals, included a specific pledge to create environmental sustainability. 2007 marked the halfway point in the world's effort to achieve these goals, and while progress has been impressive in some places, we're nowhere close to halfway there. President Bush and other world leaders made bold commitments, but many of them have yet to be realized. How can the United States help put the world back on track?

First, our nation should make good on the promises it has made to expand foreign aid targeted at fighting poverty, cancel the debts of poor countries and seek fairer international-trade rules that allow people living in poverty to empower themselves in the fight against poverty.

Second, our nation's leaders should recognize the emerging consensus that we can no longer ignore our role in safeguarding the health and balance of God's creation. We must take seriously our share in the global responsibility for reducing carbon emissions, and work with other nations to provide the resources and technology transfers that will allow poor countries to address their energy needs through clean-energy sources that will not hasten the rate of climate change.

Of course, it is not the United States alone that needs to deliver. When leaders of the G8 meet in early June [2007] in Germany, climate change will be at the top of their agenda. The health and well-being of Africa is also on the agenda, but much further down. Now is an ideal time for Americans to write, call, or e-mail the president and urge him to work with other leaders in the G8 to consider climate change and deadly poverty side-by-side as facets of the same problem. The good news is that Americans are getting involved like never before. Faith communities such as the Episcopal Church, from which I come, are organizing in communities all over the country, as are citizens from many other walks of life. Millions of Americans have joined the call for comprehensive solutions to poverty through efforts like ONE: The Campaign to Make Poverty History, and groups like the U.N. Millennium Campaign are working with citizens in all parts of the world. To be successful, though, the effort needs even more voices. It needs all of us.

At the very beginning of the Judeo-Christian Scriptures, we hear of God's creation of the universe and his proclamation that the whole of it is very good. Ultimately, this story is an account of relationships: the bond of love between God and the world, and the interconnectivity of all people and all things in that world. It is only when we take seriously those relationships—when we realize that all people have a stake in the health and well-being of all others and of the Earth itself—that creation can truly begin to realize the abundant life that God intends for every one of us.

# —4—

# *To Save This Fragile Earth*

## *The Very Reverend Samuel T. Lloyd III*

*The Very Reverend Dr. Samuel T. Lloyd III is the ninth Dean of the Washington National Cathedral. Previously, he was rector of Trinity Church, one of the largest churches in Boston, Massachusetts. He holds a Ph.D. in English Literature from the University of Virginia and a Doctor of Divinity from Virginia Theological Seminary. He is a regent of the University of the South, and a trustee of Episcopal Media Center. He is on the Board of Ministry at Harvard University. He has been published in several Anglican publications. He is a veteran of the U.S. Air Force.*

I didn't think spring was ever going to come. I mean it. Never. Maybe it was the temperature on Easter Day, which as someone pointed out was five degrees colder than it had been on Christmas Day. Or maybe it has been these past weeks of April when a gray chill, wind, and rain greeted us anytime we ventured outdoors. But it's here. Daffodils have yielded to tulips. Leaves have returned to the trees' skeletons. The grass is green again, and the blossoms and flowers are everywhere. I remember when I lived in Boston a friend saying that in New England spring comes in like a Yankee lady—reserved, proper, slow to reveal her charms. But in the South, spring comes in like a hussy—brash, flashy, showing off. I'm glad to say that Washington has all the signs of a Southern spring!

To see the earth come alive around here is to be dazzled. It must be what the poet Gerard Manley Hopkins felt a century ago when he gazed around at spring bursting out and wrote, "What is all this juice and joy?" And the words of another Hopkins poem leap to mind on a day like this:

> The world is charg'd with the grandeur of God
> It will flame out, like shining from shook foil.

The rebirth of spring has for centuries been associated in the Northern Hemisphere with Easter. Even the word "Easter" comes from the name of an Anglo-Saxon goddess of spring. Christians have seen in the return of life to nature an image of God's triumph over everything that dies. In the flowering dogwood and rhododendron we can see pointers to the power that moves through all creation bringing life out of death.

The earth comes alive, and that is itself a sort of miracle. But today as we gather here on this Earth Day we have to face the fact that that miracle is terrifyingly fragile, and that "this fragile earth, our island home," as our Prayer Book calls it, is in deep trouble.

Scientists have suspected for more than twenty years that our planet is warming as a result of carbon dioxide being released into the atmosphere from burning coal, gas, and oil. And a decade ago scientific experts were already saying that global warming is the largest challenge civilization faces, but at the time the evidence was still fragmentary, and they also thought the warming would happen gradually. But two things have happened in the last few years. One is that the evidence has become overwhelming that warming is happening and that human beings are the cause, and the second is the conviction that the change is happening far faster than anyone had imagined.

We have read in the newspapers the reports of the Intergovernmental Panel on Climate Change, bringing together the research of a thousand scientists from seventy-four countries. They declared that global warming is already affecting the Earth's ecosystems, and that climate change could lead to widespread drought and to vast flooding of coastal cities driving hundreds of millions of people from their homes. It could lead to the extinction of as much as a third of the plant and animal species, to widespread malnutrition and disease. The years 2005 and 2006 were, they reported, the hottest in recorded history.

We've been seeing indications of global warming steadily in the news—the melting ice caps on mountains, the shrinking glaciers, the increasing incidence of coastline cities underwater. A few years ago, The New York Times ran on its front page a picture of an Indonesian village now finding itself inundated as water levels rise. James Hansen, the country's foremost climatologist who has for years as a NASA researcher run the most powerful computer model on the climate, has said that we have a decade to reverse the flow of carbon into the atmosphere or else we will live, and these are his words, on a "totally different planet."

And then a group of senior military generals warned that global warming poses a major security threat. It will bring chaos, civic strife, genocide, and the growth of terrorism in Asia, Africa, and the Middle East. "We will pay for this one way or another," General Zinni said—by reducing greenhouse gas emissions today or with military conflict and loss of human lives later.

In short, we are facing what is being called a "planetary emergency."

"So what?" many might say. Things may get a little warmer here in the U.S., but chances are if we don't live along the coastlines, we may not be hit too badly. But what kind of response is that? What we are learning is that our human choices, and mainly the choices of the most wealthy nations in the world, are endangering our fragile earth and the well-being of hundreds of millions of people, and we, you and I, are part of the problem.

Every now and then I have the privilege of holding an infant, or having a wide-ranging conversation with a three-year-old. When I think of those youngsters, I can't help but wonder what are we doing to the world they will live in, and even more, to the kind of world their children will live in. We are squandering a sacred birthright that has been entrusted to us. We are participating in a massive time of decreation—tearing down mountains to produce coal, spewing poison into the atmosphere, leveling forests that are the purifying lungs our planet needs to breathe. And for what?

The United States, with 4 percent of the world's population, is producing 25 percent of the greenhouse gases that are endangering our world. But we are so addicted to a standard of living and a way of life built on inexpensive oil and coal that we don't want to begin to imagine a way out.

Writer Bill McKibben puts the issue clearly: "If you care about social justice, this is the biggest battle we've ever faced." Climate change may produce hundreds of millions of refugees. He describes wandering through the lowlands of Bangladesh, the home to 150 million and contemplating their entire homeland going under water—and these are a people who have done nothing to create the problem.

It's enough to make us think again of Gerard Manley Hopkins' poem where, after singing of God's grandeur, he describes what we have done to this glorious earth:

> All is seared with trade; bleared, smeared with toil;
> And wears man's smudge and shares man's smell.

We humans are on the verge of doing irreparable damage to the nest that bears all of our lives. I continue to be haunted by that 1969 photograph we all know of the earth when it was first viewed from outer space. There it was, a beautiful blue globe, with its swirls of white clouds, floating through the fathomless dark night of space. James Irwin, one of the astronauts who first saw that sight, said, "This beautiful, warm living object looked so fragile, so delicate, that if you touched it with a finger it would crumble and fall apart. Seeing this has changed [us]." Only it hasn't.

You will continue to hear a great deal in the coming years about this crisis from the media, environmentalists, and, I hope, our political leaders. But today we are asking what this crisis means to us as Christians. We Christians believe that, as the Psalmist puts it, "The earth is the Lord's, and all that is in it." Some have called this the Eleventh Commandment. The earth is God's, not ours. We are called to be stewards of it, to care for it lovingly, and to hand it on no worse than we found it.

But of course Christians have too often been part of the problem. Beginning in the earliest centuries, Christian faith started emphasizing an otherworldly salvation, and the whole point of faith was to deliver us from the world. In fact there was a study a few years ago that reported that the more religious people are, the less they are inclined to care about the environment. Maybe the most famous example of that was former Secretary of the Interior in the 1980s James Watt, a fundamentalist Christian who said that long range conservation of natural resources was unnecessary because Jesus would be coming soon to end everything, and so it wasn't worth it.

But the deepest Christian instincts have been defined by Jesus, as in our gospel when he points to the lilies of the field and the ravens in the air as models for simple trust in God. And in the parable of The Rich Young Man (Matthew 19:16–30), Jesus pointed to the destructiveness of piling up more and more wealth.

And it was St. Francis who saw the creation as an array of blood relatives—brother sun, sister moon, brother wind, sister water, mother earth. "Be praised, my Lord God," he said, "in and through your creation." There is one life in all of God's creatures.

The farmer, poet, novelist Wendell Berry says we all live within what he calls the "Great Economy,"—the economy of nature. And we must learn to fit harmoniously into this larger whole. Remember, he says, only nature knows how to make water, air, forests, and topsoil. And now we humans are destroying this "Great Economy," tearing apart the harmony we were made for.

Finding that life-giving balance calls for facing down our massive need to own bigger houses and drive ever bigger cars. It means rethinking our taste for strawberries flown in from California and apples from New Zealand. It means learning to shape lives less dependent on countless hours driving on highways. It means more energy-efficient homes and office buildings.

But unfortunately none of this is likely to make enough difference in the face of this planetary emergency. The answer will have to be public, political, governmental. We Christians need to be prepared to advocate, to educate, and to protect this fragile earth.

That will call for a massive shift in national priorities, with leadership as strong as that which led us through the Second World War, that put a man on the moon, that conquered polio, and that established basic civil rights for everyone. It will take saying no to the powerful economic interests tied up in the way things currently are. It will cost us to do this work of reconciliation with our planet earth. Are we as a nation and a world capable of that? I don't know, but I worry.

And what I do know is that I don't want to have to explain to my grandchildren or to God how we sat by, too addicted to our American way of life, to change our economy and our way of living before disasters struck.

We are being called, in how we live, how we act, and how we vote, to protect this earth we have been given. It's the Eleventh Commandment. "The Earth is the Lord's and all that is in it." The challenge we face is daunting. But the Easter promise is that God can bring life out of this threatening death. The God who raised Jesus from the dead can raise us from something less than life—our driven, wasteful lives—to life itself, a life that is simpler, more connected to the Great Economy of nature, more rooted in its place, and more committed to renewing and caring for this vulnerable nest, this fragile earth.

Even Gerard Manley Hopkins, who so mourned the

desecration of the land in his time, held on to this Easter trust that God's Spirit can kindle and renew us. His poem about God's grandeur and what we have done to it ends this way:

> And for all this, nature is never spent;
> There lives the dearest freshness deep down things;
> And though the last light off the black West went
> Oh, morning, at the brown brink eastward, springs—
> Because the Holy Ghost over the bent
> World broods with warm breast and with, Ah, bright wings.

That's the promise. The Spirit is moving in our world now to renew the face of the earth. The question is, "Will we join in?"

# And the Earth Is Filled With the Breath of Life

## *Rabbi Arthur Waskow, Ph.D.*

*Rabbi Arthur Waskow earned a Ph.D. in U.S. History from the University of Wisconsin. He is director of The Shalom Center (http://www.theshalomcenter.org), which voices a new progressive agenda in Jewish, multi-religious, and American life. He is co-author of* The Tent of Abraham, *author of* Godwrestling — Round 2, Down-to-Earth Judaism, *and a dozen other books on Jewish thought and practice, as well as books on US public policy. He is editor of* Trees Earth & Torah *and* Torah of the Earth *(2 vols). In 2007,* Newsweek *named him one of the fifty most influential American rabbis. To receive the weekly on-line Shalom Report, go to http://www.theshalomcenter.org/subscribe.*

The wisdom of the Jewish people cannot heal the earth alone, but there are unique wisdoms and unique energies that we can bring to this healing. In doing so, we can renew the deepest and most powerful energies of Judaism, energy that has been embanked and hidden so long that we don't even know it's there. In the ensuing coolness, we have ourselves cooled to large areas of Torah that can reawaken to us if we can discover them, get the coverings off.

In the deepest origins of Jewish life, the most sacred relationship was the relationship with the earth. Ancient Israel got in touch with God by bringing food to the Holy Temple. We use a most abstract term to describe this, the "sacrificial system," but it was food—all the foods of the Land of Israel. And so we affirmed, not in words but with our bodies, "We didn't invent this food; it came from a Unity of which we are a part. The earth, the rain, the sun, the seed, and our work—together, *adam* and *adamah*, the earth and human earthlings, grew this food. It came from the Unity of Life; so we give back some of it to that great Unity."

Through food and with the earth, not through words, was how biblical Jews got in touch with God. And in turn there was a way of relating to the earth that was not only working the earth or making the earth work, but resting with the earth. The tradition affirmed the earth's restfulness and the restfulness of human beings in relation to the earth. Not only the seventh-day Shabbat, but the *shmitah* year, the sabbatical year. Every seventh year the earth was entitled to rest and the human community that worked the earth was obligated to rest as well.

Shabbat—the day and the year—was one of the most powerful ways in which the community affirmed the Unity of all. That rhythm of work and rest, and that affirmation of what connects *adam* and *adamah*, the humans and the humus, the earth and the earthlings, affirmed that we live in a world of All, a world of joyfulness, spiritually together. There really was a down-to-earth Judaism.

The question is, what does it mean to us, who have lived through the Diaspora experience? It is not that we have lived only in cities—there were even Jewish farmers—but we have had a limited share of the responsibility for dealing with the earth, because we were usually not in a position of power to shape the economic or environmental policy of the communities we lived in.

What does it mean for us living in the Diaspora now? We live in a modernity in which the human race has created technology and a work system that is the most brilliant act of work in all of human history—new forms of controlling the earth, dominating the earth, making, doing, inventing. We have already affected the planet in ways no human beings—indeed, no species living on the planet—ever have before. We have changed the biology and chemistry of the planet. The only previous commensurate level of change came from outside, from the great meteor strike, 65 million years ago. Now one of the earth's own species, one that evolved with the technological ability, the intellectual ability, and the consciousness to review and improve its own work ability, has begun to affect the entire planet.

We must strive to understand what this means for us. We must open ourselves to the larger meaning of this event: Why is this happening to us? And we must also seek to reopen the wisdom of the shepherds, farmers, and tree-keepers that we were a couple of thousand years ago.

First, my own thoughts on how to think Jewishly about why this is happening to us. Some Kabbalists have taught that an Infinite and Utterly unfettered God, One Who encompassed all that was and wasn't, is and isn't, contracted inward in order to leave space for a universe to emerge. But in that empty space, what was the seed of the world? It was the "leftovers" of God, the thin film, as it were, of olive oil that is left within a vessel when one pours the oil out. It was this thin film of God that grew and grew, appearing as the universe—itself indeed the universe, God disguised by folds of God into seeming something other than God. And this aspect of God grows toward revealing Itself, toward mirroring the Infinite Beyond.

This growth, this process of self-revelation and self-mirroring of the God Whose Name is *Ehyeh asher Ehyeh*, "I Will Be Who I Will Be," makes up all that we may see of evolution and history. This growth appears to us as a double spiral: one spiral of increasing power intertwined with another spiral of increasing love, one spiral of rising I-It intertwined with another of broadening I-Thou, one spiral of more Doing intertwined with one of deeper Being. Each of these comes into the world as a step in the journey of the world to become more and more a Mirror for God, more and more a fully aware being, ever more fully aware of its own Unity,

The emergence of life was one enormous leap forward in the ability of aspects of the universe to understand and control, and then of these same aspects to pause, reflect, love, and be self-aware.

The emergence of the human race was another such great step. For the universe to continue on this journey toward self-awareness, there needs to be a species capable of self-awareness—made up of individuals who can reflect upon their own selves, and also able as a species to reflect upon itself and to see itself as part of the Unity of the universe—on which it is also capable of reflecting. That is what it means to live in the Image of God—to reflect upon the Unity, and thus to mirror God's Own Self. Among the species on this planet, the human race therefore bears the Image of God—the self-awareness of Unity—most fully.

And within human history, the pastoral and agricultural revolutions were further leaps forward in accessing the Divine attributes of power. Each meant that human beings were able to hold and use powers that previously had been held only by Divine "outsiders"—gods, spirits, God. Each meant that some aspect of Divine power became more available to human hands. And so the thin film of God that became the universe revealed Itself more and more fully, as the universe grew toward mirroring the Infinite.

And on each of these occasions, a leap forward in power and control had to be followed by a broadening of love and a deepening of self-aware reflection. Otherwise the new intensity of power would have swallowed up the world. And each growth of broader community gave the context and the impetus for another leap forward in Doing, Making, I-It. Thus the double spiral continued.

The agricultural revolution was one such turn on the Doing, I-It spiral—and it required the emergence of biblical Israel, Buddhism, and the other great ancient traditions on the Being, I-Thou spiral. The last great turn on the Doing, I-It spiral came when Hellenism brought a more powerful form of economics, science, politics, and war to the Mediterranean basin. This leap shattered biblical Judaism as well as other traditional cultural and religious forms. The "I-Thou" response was the creation of Rabbinic Judaism, Christianity, and Islam.

In the last several hundred years, we have been living through another such leap forward in the I-It powers of the human race. This leap is what we call modernity. It is by far the greatest of these leaps, for it brings the human race into the arena in which it is transforming the web of life from which it sprang.

That we would reach this point was probably inevitable. For to be capable of "self-awaring" life inevitably also means to be capable of creating the technology that can wreck the planet. (Our self-awareness gives us the ability to look at our technology, see its shortcomings, imagine a more effective solution, and make it happen. All life does this at some level—it is the "competitive natural selection" aspect of evolution. The mistake of "social darwinists" is to see this as the only aspect of evolution, ignoring the I-Thou spiral. Human social history is simply incomparably swifter at applying self-awareness to technological improvement—so swift that it reaches the asymptote of possible self-destruction.)

That swiftness, to some extent throughout human history but with utter urgency today, gives the human race a mandate unique among all species: to act as if it were a steward for the planet. If we fail in this task, the planet's ruination will take us with it. In that sense, we are strange stewards, for we remain partially embedded in the earth we steward.

What is the alternative to ruination? It is another curve forward on the spiral of Being, Loving, I-Thouing. It is the renewal and transformation of Judaism, Christianity, Islam, Buddhism, Hinduism, the spiritual traditions of all indigenous peoples—a renewal and transformation that can deepen each tradition in its own uniqueness while broadening the circle of love it can encompass. It is the bringing of restfulness and reflectiveness to a deeper level, just as work has been brought by modernity to a higher level. It is extending our love to the whole of the earth of which we are a part, without denying our uniqueness in its web of life.

Now that we live in the era of high-tech industrialism, and are not shepherds or farmers or foresters in the ordinary sense, we must learn to be shepherds, farmers, tree-keepers again in a different sense. For shepherds, farmers, and orchard-keepers knew you must not exhaust the earth you live on. If you're a shepherd and you let the sheep eat all the grass in one year, the sheep may be fatter and the wool thicker, but you're finished off. And farmers, vintners, and orchard-keepers learn the same thing.

What does this mean for us who have forgotten it—in the wild rush of making, doing, inventing, producing over the last couple of hundred years? What does it mean for us to renew that shepherds' wisdom, the wisdom which knew that consuming what comes from the earth is a central sacred act—is a way of being in touch with God? What would it mean for us to renew that wisdom?

I want to imagine a new version of the Jewish people—a new way of understanding and shaping ourselves. Imagine that we were to decide to see ourselves as having a mission, a purpose on the earth. A purpose to heal the earth—one that is not brand new but is described in the Torah as one of the great purposes of the Jewish people.

What does it mean that Shabbat is a symbol, a sign between the God of the universe and "His" once whole people? The Shabbat of Sinai comes in two different guises. In Exodus, we hear it as the moment when our restfulness connects us with the cosmic resting that imbues all of creation. In Deuteronomy, Shabbat renews the liberation of human beings and the earth. And there is also the Shabbat that comes before Sinai—the Shabbat that comes with the manna in the Wilderness, betokening our free and playful reconnection with the earth. This Shabbat betokens the peace agreement ending the primordial war between ourselves and earth which began as we left Eden—which came from a misdeed of eating and brought us painful toil and turmoil in our eating.

What would it mean for us to renew the sense that deep in our very covenant, deep in our covenant-sign Shabbat, is the call to be healers of the earth?

Imagine the Jewish people as a kind of transgenerational, transnational "movement," committed for seven generations, from one generation to the next and beyond, to transmit the wisdom and the practice that can heal the earth. Imagine a people that can reach out to others and can encourage others, work with others, to do that.

I want to suggest four dimensions of a Jewish people through which we could be pursuing that mission to heal the earth. These four dimensions, correspond to the four worlds through which our Kabbalists, our mystics, saw Creation.

One dimension is the explicit celebration of the Spirit through the rituals, the ceremonies, the symbols of celebration that we use to get in touch with the One. This is the world of Spirit. Look, for example, at the second paragraph of the *Sh'ma*, the one that says, "And if you act on Torah then the rain will fall, the rivers will run, and the earth will be fruitful and you will live well. And if you don't act on Torah, if you reject it, if you cut yourself off from this great harmony of earth, then the great harmony will cease to be harmony and will cut itself off from you, and the rains won't fall [or, I would say, they will turn to acid], and the rivers won't run [or they and the oceans will flood], and the sky itself will become your enemy [as in the shattering of the ozone layer or the 'CO2-ing' of the atmosphere] and you will perish from all this good *adamah* that you grew up with."

Today we can see this as a searing truth. Yet in many of our synagogues and *havurot* this passage is said in an undertone or even omitted. What would it mean for us to elevate it to a central place in our liturgy, and perhaps every four weeks or so, perhaps on the Shabbat before the new moon or the Shabbat before the full moon, to read it with a fanfare: to remind ourselves that we are part of the web of life, its most conscious part, the part most aware of the Wholeness of which we and all the rest are part—but still a part of the web, endangered whenever we bring danger on the web?

We need to focus on the second paragraph of the *Sh'ma*. By racing through it, we race through a central place of our celebration and a central place in our lives; we blind ourselves to the world around us, racing through a wonderful ecosystem without pausing to see its rich intertwining.

Let me take another example. I wrote a piece that appeared in several American Jewish newspapers in the early 1990s. It began with a fantasy. One day in the fall, all over North America, tens of thousands of Native Americans show up at the edge of rivers everywhere. They are carrying a sacred object of their own tradition, and they are also carrying willow branches. They dance seven times around their sacred symbol; they beat the willow branches on the earth; and they invoke the Holy Spirit and ask for help to heal the planet from plague and disaster and drought.

It would be on the front pages of every American newspaper and on the evening news of every television network. Everywhere students on college campuses would be demanding courses on Native American spirituality. And members of Congress and presidents of corporations would be bombarded by letters, "You mean something's wrong with the rivers, what are you doing about it?"

Now imagine a different fantasy—that it wasn't tens of thousands of Native Americans, but tens of thousands of

American Jews who showed up on this day in the fall. Their sacred object was the Torah, and they danced around it and they beat willow branches on the earth, and they prayed in English and Hebrew for the energy to heal the earth. They too appeared on television, and they too led demands that Congress and the corporations heal the earth.

What would many of our present Jewish leaders say?— No doubt, "This is primitive, this is pagan, this is radical, this is un-Jewish!"

Yet what I have just described is at the end of most traditional Jewish prayer books, because it's a description of the seventh day of Sukkot, Hoshanah Rabbah. But we don't do it anymore, we certainly don't do it that way. A few people in some traditional synagogues will gather in a small chapel and beat willow branches on the rug. Nobody ever hears about it. And they say the words of prayer to heal the earth, but they don't connect the words with any act that might be done.

Look at the prayerbooks, however, look up Hoshanah Rabbah, the seventh day of the festival of Sukkot, and look at the words of "*Hosha na.*" "*Hosha na*" got transliterated into the rather meaningless English word "hosanna"—it actually means "Please save us." Right there: "Save the earth, save us!" And read the words of these prayers, for almost all of them name the dangers that face the earth and plead with the Breath of all life to save the earth from plague and drought.

Those are just two examples; the tradition is rich with possibilities. Our whole festival cycle, after all, is attuned to the rhythms of the earth. Let us imagine it alive with earth again:

• On Tu B'Shvat, the festive New Year of the Trees that comes at the full moon of deep winter, we can plant the trees that together make up the Tree of Life. (In the Headwaters redwood forest of California, two hundred Jews actually trespassed on the land of a corporation that was threatening to log those grand and sacred groves, so old they were living when the Temple fell. It was Tu B'Shvat; we planted redwood seedlings.)

• At Pesach we can eliminate the swollen *chameytz* (leavening) that makes our lives swell up, and embrace instead a week of simple living. And at Pesach we can identify the pharaonic institutions that are bringing upon us the plagues that turn our seas and rivers to "red tide," that fill our cattle with disease, that infest one or another ecosystem of the earth with swarms of invasive species that destroy a habitat. We can call on these corporate pharaohs to open their hearts instead of hardening them, and to save the land they are destroying.

• And we can face not only the dark side of Pesach, the *chameytz* and the plagues, but we can also read together the Song of Songs, that lovely evocation of a spring in which humanity at last learns how to live in loving, playful peace with all of earth as well as with each other.

For us to celebrate our ancient festivals in such ways, however, to pray such "*Hosha nas*," we would have to be convinced of their wisdom and their truth, of our own authenticity in so invoking them. We would have to believe that our prayerful pleas do not fall into emptiness but into a Place that hears and can respond. In short, we would have to understand God in such a way that such prayers have meaning not only to a distant disembodied Mystery, but also to an embodiment of holiness on earth. We would have to believe, really believe, that the great

Unity includes the processes of the earth. One of the great Hasidic Rebbes, the Rebbe of Chernobyl, about two hundred years ago said, "What is the world? The world is God, wrapped in robes of God so as to appear to be material. And who are we? We are God wrapped in robes of God and our task is to unwrap the robes and to discover, uncover, that we are God."

So, think of the earth as one aspect of God, and think what it would mean for us to pray those prayers with that Hassidic understanding. We pray them, but can we act on them? As Rabbenu Heschel, our teacher Abraham Joshua Heschel, said when he came back from the civil rights march in Selma, Alabama, "I felt my legs were praying."

What would it mean for us to pray not only with our mouths but also with our arms and legs? Or, to put it another way: if earth is Spirit, then politics may be the deepest prayer, and prayer the deepest politics. We may realize that we are always choosing between a politics that may be prayers to idols, mere carved-out pieces of the Whole, things of partial value that we elevate to ultimates, and a politics that we may shape with such deep caring that it becomes prayer to the One.

The Kabbalists taught us that the process of Creation involved a great outpouring of Divine energy so intense that this river of Divinity crashed through each vessel intended to contain it, swept over four great waterfalls, Four Worlds of the Divine Flow, shattering Itself until it came to a shattered calmness in our world.

The world we have been exploring, the world of ritual and celebration, is our way of experiencing the First World, *Atzilut*, "Being," the world of Spirit.

Just below *Atzilut*, on the next water-level of the Divine river, is the Second of the Four Worlds, another dimension of what it would mean to shape from Jewish peoplehood a transgenerational movement to heal the earth. This second World is *Briyyah*, Intellect, Knowing, Learning. This involves learning Torah, and learning science, and learning public policy, and especially learning how all these intertwine.

Suppose we learn Torah simply because it was written down once upon a time, a matter of "religion" that teaches only about prayer and ceremonial. And suppose we learn science by going to a university department, politics and public policy from yet another university department or from the mass media. Then what do these three have to do with each other? Nothing, or very little.

But that's not in fact what Torah was. It was a celebration of the great unity; therefore it was politics, and it was also science, the best science available to every generation of Jews who were encoded into the process. So, when the Jubilee chapter of Leviticus (Lev 25) instructs us to let the fields lie fallow every seventh year, some guy with a master's degree in Business Administration is going to say to you, "If you let the fields lie fallow on the seventh year, what do you think we are going to eat?" The Torah says, "Hang on! You will have more to eat, I promise you, if you let the earth rest every seventh year than if you try to work it to death." Of course, this is religion. It is also science, the science that knows that the fields are more fruitful if they have a chance to lie fallow. This is not something separate from science. It affirms what is holy in the world, and what is holy includes knowledgeable science.

And this process did not stop with the Torah, or the biblical period. The rabbis of the Talmud proclaimed that no one should herd "small cattle"—that is, goats and sheep—in the Land of Israel. Why? Because they destroy trees and grass.

The rabbis say this even though they know perfectly well that our forebears were shepherds and goat herders. Why do they make such an amazing departure from tradition? Because their experience, and their science, have taught them something new. Their deep sense that our relationship with the earth is sacred causes them to oppose what was normal for the early Torah period. The basic values continue; how to affirm them changes in accord with new scientific information.

Today, we might imagine saying to ourselves: "Our Torah forbids us to cut down fruit trees, even in time of war. Today we know that every tree gives oxygen to the web of life, and great forests are crucial to the life of the entire planet. Does that mean that we may cut down any tree only if it is possible to replace its fruitful supply of oxygen? That we may not cut down great forests at all? That this is now Torah because we understand the science of trees in ways our forebears did not (though they certainly knew trees were important to their lives), and we uphold the values that they held?"

We can think such thoughts and ask such questions only if we begin to interweave the knowledge that in the modern age has been separated into religion, science, and politics. What would it mean for us to take the lines of Torah in Leviticus 26—which are incredibly powerful as both a sacred and a scientific statement, not two separate things—the lines that ask, "And what happens if you don't let the earth make its Shabbos year?" and answer, "The earth gets to rest anyway—on your head. The earth gets to rest through exile, disaster, desolation. The earth gets to rest, that is the law of gravity. The only question is if you are going to rest with it and celebrate the rest and take new life, or if the earth is going to expel you from its midst so it can rest."

This understanding was both sacred and scientific three

thousand years ago, and it still is. Today, when ecologists say, "If you insist on pouring $CO_2$ into the atmosphere and never letting the atmosphere rest from that overdose, there is going to be global warming and your civilization is going to be knocked awry if not shattered," they are simply saying what Leviticus 26 said.

What would it mean for us, both children and adults, to intertwine that learning, to shape our Torah study so that it always includes those knowledges about the web of life? What would it mean for us to reshape every Jewish curriculum and study group as if the web of life in which we live were the most important sacred fact about our lives?

Let us turn to the third dimension, the Third of the Four Worlds, the world of Relationship. For indeed the Jewish community, acting on its own, cannot heal the world. I could say to myself all day, "Hey, every time you drive the car, you are polluting the planet and bringing on global warming"—and yet if my society is set up so that the only way I can get from where I live to where I work is to drive, and there are no bike paths, and mass transit is rare, run down, and expensive—then I am going to feel guilty but I am going to drive the car. It does not help the planet if I feel guilty.

In other words, we have to act with other peoples and other communities to shape a society where we can walk from where we work to where we sleep, or we can bike, or we can take mass transit that is far more efficient and less wasteful, and less likely to damage the atmosphere. And we have to draw on the energy and clout of the Jewish people, our new ability in the Diaspora to make a difference in the societies we are a part of.

One of the notions that has arisen in American society

in the last twenty years is the idea that acting to heal the earth means acting to damage ordinary people, that there is, for example, a war between owls and timber workers, and any law advancing the owls hurts the timber workers.

Recent American politics, however, has shown that the enemies of the owls and of the timber workers are the same— they are the institutions that see it as their task to gobble up the planet. To gobble it up biologically, to gobble it up culturally by destroying small communities which just don't fit, and to gobble up local and regional economies that just don't fit into the global market economy. To gobble up the kinds of enterprises where owners and workers felt responsible to each other, where even in the midst of struggles, management and labor unions felt some kind of responsibility, a sense of limits of what profits could be, a sense of limits on whether you can fire tens of thousands of people in a prosperous, profitable company. The new corporations of Modernity Amok destroy such companies: their profits could be bigger; in this way regional and local economies are shattered along with local cultures and local bio-regions, ecosystems.

Gobbling the globe means chewing up living creatures, thousands of species. It means chewing up small, odd cultures: the Jews of Eastern Europe, the natives of the Amazon Valley, the Shoshone. It means chewing up the local factory neighborhoods in Philadelphia, even the IBM towns of upstate New York. It means chewing up the family in all its forms.

The institution of Global Gobble is the global corporation, and its Torah says that producing is what human life is all about. Producing—and of course consuming, which is not the opposite of producing, but only the other side of the coin (and I do mean coin). In the Torah of the global corporation, resting, celebrating, reflecting, loving, being there, are all a waste of time, literally. Shabbat, a waste of time!! Think what you could be making if you were not resting!

That attitude toward the earth becomes also an attitude toward human beings. It creates a technology that pushes people in two directions: either being disemployed because the technology is better, more efficient; or keeping their jobs, but being forced to match their lives to the speed of the machine.

The result is that more and more people who keep their jobs don't work eight-hour days, but ten-, twelve-, or even fourteen-hour days. And people who lose their jobs scrabble together two, three, even four jobs in order barely to hold on by their fingertips.

In the process, community is dying, divided between the disemployed and the overworked. The overworked have no time for family or neighborhood or religious life or grassroots politics. Some of the disemployed—those who end up on the streets with no work at all or in prison because they get desperate, crazy, drugged, or alcoholic— get a perverse form of leisure, but they cannot use it for family, neighborhood, religious life, or politics.

Neither the overworked nor the disemployed can get their lives together to help shape a decent society. Neither the desperate disemployed nor the exhausted overworked can shape a loving family. In their neighborhoods, the only thing you have the energy to do after a twelve-hour day is to sit in front of the television set, which takes your depressed and exhausted self and reawakens it with jolts of your own adrenaline. And then since you are feeling jangled from being awakened that way, it calms you down with "Hey, here's something wonderful to buy." So if you're exhausted or desperate you don't create PTAs, neighborhoods, synagogues, churches, or political parties.

There is a wonderful study by Robert Putnam called "Bowling Alone." The bowling leagues are disappearing; people still bowl but they bowl alone, because they don't have the energy anymore even to organize a bowling league. If this seems so unimportant as to be ridiculous even to mention, the point is that the seedbed of democracy, as De Tocqueville taught, is all those networks of local organizations.

We need to be serious about addressing both the issues of what we call the economy and what we call the environment. They are deeply intertwined. An economy is the way in which earthlings and the earth fit together.

Economy and ecology: it is no accident that they both begin with the Greek word for household; they are both about the same processes of the human relationship with the earth. And those who want to heal the earth must also understand the institutional structures that are damaging the earth and also damaging our society. To act on either, we must act on both.

The Fourth World, the fourth dimension of our imagined sacred people, is the world of Doing, Action, Physicality. The world of eco-kosher. It was Rabbi Zalman Schachter-Shalomi who coined the word "Eco-Kosher." That word almost teaches its lesson in the word itself, if you let it reverberate in your head a little while. But let me unfold it just a tiny bit.

For people who were shepherds and farmers, celebrating food was the way of celebrating the crucial relationship between *adam* and *adamah*, because food was the crucial connection between them. And so our people generated not only the elaborate celebrations of that sacred nexus through the offerings of food at the Holy Temple, but also an elaborate pattern of what food to eat, and in what way: the Kosher code.

When the elaborate Temple offerings were no longer possible, the rabbis of the Talmud compensated by making the rules of Kashrut even more elaborate.

In the society we live in, while food is obviously important, it is not the biggest piece of our economic relationship with the earth. It's not all we eat anymore. We eat coal. We eat oil. We eat electric power, we eat the radiation that keeps some of that electric power going, and we eat the chemicals that we turn into plastic. What does it mean to eat them in a sacred way? What does it mean to say that we're Eco-Kosher? What does it mean to apply more broadly the basic sense of Kashrut that what you eat and how you eat it matters?

Today our most dangerous addictive substances are not heroin, or nicotine, or alcohol. They are plutonium and petroleum. These are social addictions, not individual ones. I do not mainline oil or gasoline into my own body's veins, but America mainlines gasoline into our society's veins.

What is addiction? It is feeling unable to control or limit a behavior, especially using a substance—even one that in some limited uses may be beneficial—in such a way as to receive immediate pleasure at the high risk of long-run disease and death. And that describes America's relationship to gasoline.

Addictions are to a great extent a spiritual problem— what in ancient Jewish language was called idolatry. Carving out a small part of the great Flow of Life and worshiping that small part. Letting it take over our lives. A serious Jewish community today should see these social addictions as idolatries; we must work out ways of infusing our use of oil, coal, paper, and all the rest with holiness. We must eat them in an Eco-Kosher way.

Is it eco-kosher to eat vegetables and fruit that have been grown by drenching the soil with insecticides?

Is it eco-kosher to drink the wine of Shabbat *kiddush* from throw-away non-biodegradable plastic cups? Or would it be eco-kosher to share ceramic cups; to begin each *kiddush* with the *kavvanah*, the intentional focus, that we are using these cups to heal the earth; and to end each meal with the sacred act of washing these cups so as to heal the earth? Is it eco-kosher to use electricity generated by nuclear power plants that create waste products that will remain poisonous for fifty thousand years?

Is it eco-kosher to ignore the insulation or lack of it in our homes, synagogues, community centers, and nursing homes, so that we burn far more fuel than necessary and drunkenly pour carbon dioxide into the atmosphere, thereby accelerating the heating of our globe?

Is it eco-kosher to use 100 percent unrecycled office paper and newsprint in our homes, our synagogues, our community newspapers? Might it be eco-kosher to insist on 10 percent recycled paper this year, and 30 percent in two years, and 80 percent in five years?

I want to suggest that what makes a life-practice eco-kosher may not be a single standard, a black-white barricade like "Pork is *treyf*"—but rather a constantly moving standard in which the test is: Are we doing what is more respectful, less damaging to the earth than what we did last year?

What would it mean to evolve a code of daily Jewish practice for how we consume, how we eat all these things that come from *adamah*? What would it mean for each Hillel, each congregation, each Jewish Community Center and nursing home, to review what kind of paper, what kind of energy it uses? Do we invest money in industries that destroy the earth, or industries that heal the earth? Most of the Jewish community is not asking those questions yet. What must we do, then, to begin the creation of Eco-Kashrut?

I have suggested four dimensions. First, the Spirit: what we call ritual, ceremony, prayer, celebration, the direct ways of getting in touch with that sense of unity, of allness in the world. Second, Knowledge: the kind of education that intertwines our ancient tradition with the constantly growing edges of tradition, with knowledge in all the spheres of relationship between human beings and the earth. Third, Relationship: reaching out to other communities and societies everywhere to join with us to heal the wounded earth. And fourth, Doing: the daily eco-kosher practice of our own self, of our households, and our community organizations.

These four need to be treated not as four separate parts but as aspects of the One. When they are split apart, very little happens. In most synagogues today, if issues of the earth are dealt with at all they are broken up in separate spheres. Issues of the earth and ritual are discussed within the ritual committee; issues of the earth and knowledge are discussed within the education committee; issues of the earth in everyday practice are dealt with in the house committee that decides what paper is bought or who comes in to check the insulation; issues of society are dealt with by the social action committee. In each of those committees, however, the issue of how to deal with the relationship to the earth, is probably third or fourth or fifth on the list of priorities. Perhaps on one committee the issue of the earth will come forward, but on the next front where the issue must be addressed, the specific committee is not interested, and the question molders.

We should not let this happen. The issue of the earth is such that in a unique way, all these in fact are intertwined.

So I think perhaps the crucial strategic switch in any Jewish community, congregation or organization comes when that community decides to create an *Adam-and-Adamah* committee, even if it has to be called the Committee on the Environment. *Adam-and-Adamah* says, "Hey, we ain't identical but we sure are closely intertwined." You can't say *adam* without hearing *adamah*, you can't say *adamah* without hearing *adam*. The "environment" is—something else, somewhere else. But whatever we name the committee, I think the crucial change in any Jewish community or organization may be when a single *Adam-and-Adamah* body is created that has responsibility for all of those four dimensions, to report on them to the community as a whole.

From then on, judging from the places where this has already happened, things are different. The community begins to imagine itself as a piece of a broader movement to heal the earth, to imagine that that is a major aspect of what Judaism is all about.

Reframing Judaism in this way can evoke passionate commitment from the next generation of Jews, in ways that few other things can. Much of what the human race is doing to the planet will have its worst effects on the planet thirty, forty, fifty years from now. Our children will have to live in what we have created. Judaism which addresses the future of the earth will evoke their passion, energy, intelligence, commitment, and spirit. Conversely, a Judaism which says, "Hey, what's this earth stuff got to do with us?" won't fly.

The passionate engagement which comes from a sense that we fit into the great Unity, is profoundly necessary if the human race is to decide to stop gobbling up the earth. Those who are spiritually starving will need to fill their bellies with something—and they will try to fill themselves by gobbling the earth. Intense song, dance, Torah-study, drushodrama, the engagement of the whole body, the full involvement of both women and men in shaping spiritual practice—all this spiritual intensity is crucial to a recovering addict. Spiritual vitality is necessary if we are to heal the planet.

I would encourage any of you who talk with people who talk of Jewish continuity to say, "Continuity? What is its content? Because if its content is a real, alive, down-to-earth Judaism then I'm ready to put my passion into this. And if not, I will put my passion elsewhere, or perhaps I will cynically give up, and put my passion nowhere. For this is a question of life and death to me, a question of the life and death of my children who are not yet in this world. If you're not interested in my life or death, then I am not interested whether the empty Judaism you speak for lives or dies. Its continuity means nothing."

It does not have to be that way. Together we can create a Judaism that has a purpose for its continuity, a Judaism that answers the question, "What for?"

What for? For the Breath of Life Who fills the universe. For the web of life that is the universe. And here is where we share in our depth the Breath that all peoples breathe—by whatever Name they name the One Who is always becoming.

We do the breathing, and we are the Breath. All of us. Not only do the trees breathe in what we breathe out, and we breathe in what the trees breathe out, but so do all the species, all the peoples.

Shabbat did not come to us because we were "the Jews"; we became "the Jews" because we heard the silence of Shabbat. We should be welcoming others into that hearing, even as we ourselves—some of us—have had to relearn it from the breathing of yoga and the sitting of Zen and the meditating of Buddhists and the whirling of Sufis and the chanting of those who still live on Turtle Island.

It is now the restful task of all the spiritual traditions, Buddhism and Hinduism, Christianity and Islam, Judaism and Wicca, to learn from each other how to rest. To catch our Breath. To dance another turn in the great spiral of I-Thou. Together.

# —6—
# Global Warming and Health—An Islamic Concern

## Dr. Shahid Athar, M.D.

*Dr. Shahid Athar, MD, is a U.S. citizen. He is a Clinical Associate Professor at Indiana University School of Medicine. He is an endocrinologist in private practice in Indianapolis, Indiana. He is a fellow of the American College of Physicians and American College of Endocrinology. He is past president of the Islamic Medical Association of North America, and the Interfaith Alliance of Indiana (IAI). He is an author of seven books and more than 120 published articles on medical and Islamic topics. For his interfaith activities, The Indianapolis Medical Society in 2002 awarded him the Governor Otis Bowen Award for Community Service. American College of Physicians (Indiana chapter) named him a Laureate Physician in 2008 and St. Vincent Health a "Distinguished Physician" in 2009. His latest book is* Healing the Wounds of September 11, 2001. *([www.islam-usa.com](www.islam-usa.com))*

Lo! In the creation of the heavens and the earth, and the difference of the night and the day and the ships which sail in the ocean of use to men and the water that God sends down from the sky, thereby reviving the earth after its death and dispersing all kinds of animals therein and the ordinance of the clouds obedient between heaven and earth; are signs for people who reflect (Qur'an 2:164).

The natural disasters of Hurricanes Katrina and Rita and before that of the Tsunami and the earthquake in Kashmir, which affected thousands of lives, have shown us how vulnerable we humans are and how equally we suffer irrespective of our faith. The earth has been given to us as a gift from the Creator and we, the recipients of this gift, must protect and preserve it. Even though Samuel Huntington talks about "The Clash of Civilizations" in his book in which he foretells of an inevitable war between Islam and Christianity, the fact is that Abrahamic religions and all religions have much in common in view of a natural world. In the scriptures there are similar stories and ethical concepts regarding the preservation of the earth. The word earth or in Arabic, *ard*, appears no less than 485 times in Qur'an and the word *shari'ah*, Islamic law, literally means the path to water. No wonder green is the color of Islam.

Environmental statistics are well known to everyone interested in the subject. There are many websites and organizations that are dedicated to this issue. There is no doubt that global warming is taking place. An increase in global warming leads to increased water vapor and abrupt changes in climate, including hurricanes. Global warming will also lead to more infectious diseases like malaria. The United States, which has 4 percent of the world's population, is the producer of 25 percent of the world's carbon dioxide. In addition to global warming, our threats are from chemicals, fertilizers, herbicides, industrial wastes, and air pollution including smoking. There is a shortage of fresh water for human use as we use more water for industries and less for agriculture. Added to this is the question of economic injustice, the North/South debate, poverty and lack of healthcare for people who are underprivileged, not only worldwide but even in our country.

God has created everything in this universe in due proportion and measure both in quantity and quality. In the universe, there is enormous diversity and variety of form and function. In it and in various elements there are fulfillments of human welfare and evidence of the Creator's greatness. Human beings are a part of these universes, the elements of which are complementary to one another and protect each other rather than being subservient to one another. God has made water the basis of and origin of life. God says in the Qur'an, "we make from water everything." When NASA sends out missions into the universe they are looking for water as proof of life on other planets. The Qur'an 25: 48-49 says "and we send down pure water from the sky, thereby bringing life to dead land and quenching the thirst of that which we have created, cattle and man in multitude."

The message of Islam is "Mercy to Mankind" (Qur'an 21:107). The notion of mercy extends not only to human beings, but to plants as well as to the animal kingdom. It is mentioned from the stories of the life of Prophet Mohammed that once he saw a companion remove a baby pigeon from a nest. Prophet Mohammed confronted that person and gently returned the bird to its nest saying "for charity shown to each creature with a soft heart, there is a reward." It was said by an Islamic scholar that all living things are partners with humans in existence and they deserve their own respect.

Coming back to the preservation of water, Islam forbids the wastage of water and usage thereof without benefit. The industrial pollutants going through the waterways and oceans that will pollute the water and threaten marine life are forbidden in Islam. Islam also considers earth as our first mother and all mothers have their rights. Their right is that they not be violated and that they be respected. The animals also have rights and Islam forbids Muslims to kill an animal just for play. It is said that if someone kills a bird for amusement, the bird will demand justice from that person on the Day of Judgment. Jesus (peace be upon him) instructed us to "Love Thy Neighbor." In Islam, the neighbor is defined not only as fellow humans but all living beings around us.

How does all of this affect our health? God has given us clean, healthy lungs and we destroy them by smoking or inhaling second hand smoke. That is not the will of God. He has given us healthy livers and we destroy them by drinking alcohol. That is not the will of God.

We Muslims are not supposed to harm ourselves or anyone else. We know that. Religion should not be confined to acts of worship in a place of worship. The place of worship is at home and outside the churches and mosques, on the street where we go out and take care of fellow humans who are also members of our family. The Qur'an asks us to "save yourself and your family from fire." Scholars believe that the fire that is mentioned is not just hell fire, but the fires that we have created from our own actions. The Qur'an also says, "Everything good that happens to you or mankind is from God and everything bad that happens to you is by your own actions." Our own actions here are our industrial growth, material greed, and luxuries that drive us crazy and endanger not only the environment, but our own health and the health of fellow humans as well as other forms of life. "Do not create mischief on earth after it has been set in order," the Qur'an says.

## The Effects of War on the Environment

Not only does air bombing pollute the air, water, and soil, but it also has long term environmental effects. We know of the effects of Agent Orange in the VietNam war and the effects of the use of depleted uranium warheads in the Gulf War. Also, during the Gulf War many oil fields were bombed in the region and oil continued to burn for several years leading to black rain in the region which had effects on vegetation as well as caused respiratory illnesses in humans. Mountains are described in the Qur'an as firm anchors or pegs to stabilize earth (Q 13:3, 15:19, and 16:15). It is my feeling that several years of intense bombing of snow covered mountains in Afghanistan might have some geological effects related to the severe earthquake on October 8, 2005.

## Religious Accord in Environmental Ethics

The points of religious accord in environmental ethics that Muslims endorse are as follows:

1.  The natural world has value in itself and does not exist solely to serve human needs. There is a significant continuity of being between humans and non-humans, living beings, even though humans do have a distinctive role and responsibility.
2.  Non-human living beings are morally significant in the eyes of God and in the cosmic order. They have their own unique relationship to God and their own places in the cosmic order.
3.  The dependence of human life on the natural world can and should be acknowledged in the rituals and other explorations with an attitude of appreciation.
4.  Moral norms such as justice, compassion and reciprocity apply in

appropriate ways both in human beings and non-human beings. The well-being of humans and well-being of non-humans are inseparably connected.

5. There are legitimate and illegitimate uses of nature.
6. Greed and destructiveness are condemned. Restraint and protection is recommended.
7. Humans are obliged to be aware and responsible for living in harmony with the natural world and should follow specific practices for this, prescribed by their traditions.

It is well known that a high level of ozone has an impact on our health in terms of bronchitis, asthma, and other respiratory disorders. Now the question comes, "What can we do ourselves?" There is pessimism that it is the government's or industry's responsibility and we individuals can not do much ourselves. This is not true. Obviously, we can lead a healthy life, eat healthy food, give up smoking, drive less, and use fewer gas-guzzlers. Whatever we can do to preserve nature and other living beings, including plants, is an act of faith and an act of worship to the God that we profess to believe in.

Let me end with two stories to make my point. There was a boat in the ocean with two decks. The upper deck folks had all the provisions and lower deck folks had very little. In the middle of the ocean, the folks in the lower deck ran out of drinking water. So they sent one person to upper deck to ask them for some water to share. The self-centered folks in the upper deck refused to share. The thirsty folks in the lower deck had no choice but to dig a hole in the boat to get some water. Well, when the boat sank, it drowned the folks of both decks. **Friends! We are in this boat of environmental mess together. Unless we all do something to save our earth, we will have the same fate.**

Finally, there is the story of a wise man who had the correct answers to all questions asked. A person became jealous of him and challenged him. He took a small little bird in his fist and closed his fist. He thought that he would ask the wise man if the bird was alive or dead. If the wise man said it was alive then he would kill the bird and if he said bird was dead then he would open his fist and let the bird fly. In either case, the wise man would be proven wrong for the first time. The wise man was wise enough to know the trick of this wicked man. So he replied in response to the question asked, **"The fate of the bird is in your hand."**

**My friends, the fate of our Earth is in our hands.**

# —7—
# *A Christian's Case for Earth Care*

## Matthew Sleeth, M.D.
## Nancy Sleeth

*Matthew Sleeth, MD, a former emergency room physician, felt like he was straightening deck chairs on the Titanic saving one patient at a time while the whole ship (Earth) was going down. Together with his wife and two children, he began to bring his lifestyle in line with his values, cutting back on their fossil fuel consumption by two thirds and electricity use by more than nine tenths. Following a new calling, Dr. Sleeth resigned from his position as chief of the medical staff and director of the ER to teach, preach and write about faith and the environment. He is the author of,* Serve God, Save the Planet: A Christian Call to Action *(Zondervan), the introduction to the* Green Bible *(HarperOne), and* The Gospel According to the Earth: Why the Good Book is a Green Book *(HarperOne). He is a graduate of George Washington University School of Medicine and has held two post doctoral fellowships. Dr. Sleeth has been a member of the American Academy of Family Practice, the College of Emergency Physicians, and the College of Executive Physicians. He is currently the executive director of Blessed Earth (www.blessedearth.org) a faith-based nonprofit focusing on environmental stewardship.*

**The following is an excerpt taken from *Serve God, Save the Planet* by Dr. Matthew Sleeth. Copyright 2006 by Zondervan. Used by permission of Zondervan.** *www.zondervan.com*

## *A Christian's Case for Earth Care*

Many Christians are unaware of or surprised to find that prominent church leaders from all denominations are calling the rank and file to support clean air, clean water, fuel efficiency, and non-toxic manufacturing. Why is this? Let's look at one of the common arguments against personal stewardship of the earth, and then we'll look at the biblically based reasoning that supports stewardship and environmental temperance.

### God gave us dominion over everything

The beginning of Genesis describes the creation of the earth and the teeming creatures on land, sea, and air. It tells of humanity's creation and of God's willingness to give humans responsibility for nature. Contrary to some popular opinions, God gives only partial responsibility to humanity when he gives us dominion over the earth. *Dominion* comes from a Hebrew term meaning "higher on the root of a plant." Dominion does not mean ownership or even unrestricted use. Implied in our dominion is our dependency on everything under us. Cut the root out from under a plant and the fruit above will perish, despite its superior position.

When we drop off children at kindergarten, we cede dominion over them to the teacher. Without this partial transfer of responsibility, chaos would reign in a classroom. At the end of the day, when we pick up our children from school, we expect to find them in the same or better condition as when they arrived. We would not tolerate finding them battered or less intelligent at the end of the day.

I suspect that if we lent our car to a friend (i.e., gave him dominion over it), we would be very unhappy to get our car back dented, dirty, and with an empty tank. Being pro-stewardship is not a case of valuing forests more than people; rather, it means valuing human possessions less, and God's world more. Surely we must value the loan of God's earth at least as much as we value the loan of an automobile, for God's earth is on loan to each generation.

God made the heavens and the earth, and his blessings are upon all living creatures.

> And God said, Let the waters bring forth abundantly the moving creatures that have life, and fowl that may fly above the earth in the open firmament of heaven. And God created great whales, and every living creature that moveth, which the waters brought forth abundantly, after their kind, and every winged fowl after his kind; and God saw that it was good. And God blessed them . . . (Genesis 1:20–22, KJV).

When the passenger pigeon became extinct, God took note. When we exterminate a species, we forever lose dominion over it. We cancel God's blessings on a species when we destroy it. When we ignore a blessing, we show a lack of respect for God. Disrespect is blasphemous. Let us keep in our hearts this thought: God created the earth, and if we do not respect the earth and all of its creatures, we disrespect God.

*Nancy Sleeth is a graduate of Georgetown University and holds a Master's Degree in journalism. She is the author of* Go Green, Save Green: A Simple Guide to Saving Time, Money, and God's Green Earth *(Tyndale), the first ever practical guide for going green from a faith perspective. She is also the author of* The Year of Living Without: One Woman's Quest to Regain Peace and Quiet *(Tyndale, Winter 2010). Nancy is married to Matthew Sleeth, and they are the parents of Clark Sleeth, who is entering the field of missionary medicine, and Emma Sleeth, author of* It's Easy Being Green: One Student's Guide to Serving God and Saving the Planet *(Zondervan). Nancy is the Program Director of Blessed Earth.*

**The following is an article written by Nancy Sleeth and first published by Tyndale.**

## *One Family's Journey*

Afew years back, my husband was a well-respected physician at the top of his career—director of emergency services and chief of medical staff. We lived with our children, Clark and Emma, in a picture-perfect town in a three-story New England house, complete with library, guest suite, and four bathrooms. Our kids took sailing lessons in the summer and skied in the winter. We ate lobster fresh from the wharf. We were enjoying the good life and living out the American dream.

But something was missing. We had all the nice *things* that were supposed to make us happy, yet at the core we still felt hollow.

Then, during the course of one week, Matthew admitted three different women to the hospital—all in their thirties, all with breast cancer, all destined to die. One woman seized uncontrollably, and Matthew could not stabilize her. He had to go out to the waiting room and tell her husband, who had a toddler on one hip and a little girl holding his hand, that his wife was gone. Matthew did what any compassionate doctor would do: he hugged the young dad, and they cried together. That night, Matthew came home visibly upset. He told me about the young women with breast cancer, and then asked, "What are the odds?" We looked in his textbook from medical school, which said that one in nineteen women had a lifetime chance of getting breast cancer. The updated version of that same textbook said one in nine women. The incidence now, just a few years later, is nearly one in six.

Matthew said that it was time to stop "running for the cure" and start looking for the cause.

Around this time, we went on a family vacation to a barrier island off the coast of Florida. The island is idyllic—no cars, no roads, no stores—just sun and surf and beautiful sunsets. After playing in the ocean all day and running around trying to catch geckos, the kids went to bed early, exhausted. Adult time, at last! Matthew and I relaxed on the upstairs deck, watching the palm trees waving in a cool breeze and enjoying the silence of the stars. We stayed like that, just sitting in the tropical moonlight, for a long time. I couldn't help but compare the peacefulness of the night air with the busyness of our lives back home. So rarely did we have time to stop and think, to discuss the big questions of our life. Our conversation rambled from art and music, to books we were reading, to the state of the world.

And then I asked two questions that would change our lives forever.

"What do you think is the biggest problem facing the

world today?"

I could just about see the wheels whirling in Matthew's head: *Hunger? Poverty? War? AIDS?* There was no shortage of potential answers.

After a few minutes, Matthew offered a reply that I was not expecting: "The world is dying."

He explained his reasoning. "There are no chestnuts left on Chestnut Lane, no elms on Elm Street, no caribou in Caribou, Maine. The oceans are just about fished out, and the songbirds are disappearing. Rain forests the size of North Carolina are being cut down each year—and more than twenty thousand species go extinct annually." Matthew took a long sip from his glass and then sighed. "For the first time in history, the amount of living matter on earth is actually decreasing—there's no good ending to this story. If we don't have a healthy planet to sustain humanity, none of the other problems will matter."

It didn't take much to convince me that Matthew was right—our planet is indeed dying. I could see the changes in my own lifetime. As a child, I remember frequently stopping to help turtles cross the road—and seeing frogs and fireflies, honeybees and butterflies everywhere. Seemingly endless flocks of birds would fly overhead every spring and fall. But in just a few decades, nearly all of this wildlife had disappeared. The meadow behind my childhood house had been replaced with ChemLawn green grass and cookie-cutter McMansions. When I approached the nearest major city, I saw a dome of smog covering its inhabitants. Without clean air, clean water, and healthy soil our children would face a turbulent future, with people struggling for increasingly scarce resources.

The more we talked about the demise of the planet, the more depressing it all felt. The problems seemed so overwhelming. But Matthew is a big-picture thinker, a problem solver, a man of action. That's when I asked the second, more difficult, question:

"If the planet is dying, what are we going to do about it?"

My husband did not have a ready answer. But when we got back from vacation, he did not stop thinking about the challenge. A couple of months later, he finally did get back to me—with an answer I wasn't prepared to hear:

"I'll quit my job," he said, "and put all my energy toward saving the planet."

"Are you sure we need to do that much?" I replied.

I had always thought of myself as a good environmentalist. I understood why recycling was important. And picking up litter. I was even okay being the only mom on our block without a family van, making due with a more fuel-efficient sedan. But giving up a career that my husband clearly loved, as well as the prestige, steady income, and security that came along with it, to "save the planet"?

The thought terrified me. My stomach turned inside out just thinking about what we might lose—our beautiful home, our harborside neighborhood, our vacations, not to mention health benefits and a retirement plan. It wasn't like Matthew had a meaningless job—he was employed by a non-profit hospital, healing the sick and taking care of the poor. And he was extremely good at his work: Matthew had a gift for diagnosis and a talent for putting his patients at ease in even the most trying circumstances.

The selfish part of me began to whine. What about the three years of undergraduate school, four years of medical school, and three years of residency we had gone through together? Wouldn't he be wasting all that training? And then there were practical concerns: The kids were approaching their teen years. College was just around the corner. How would we possibly save enough money to pay for their education if our income dropped suddenly to zero? How, for that matter, would we put food on the table?

Each of my arguments sounded logical on its own. In the material world, my husband's sudden career change made no sense. Walking in faith may sound good in theory—when it happens to other people and everything turns out okay in the end—but I was terrified to take even the first step. What followed was a tense time, full of anxiety, fear of change, and conflicting desires.

People ask us if we had any arguments. Of course we did! I'd be lying if I said there were no raised voices or sleepless nights. But gradually I came, if not to peace, at least to acceptance of the new direction our life would take.

The transition—as much emotional and spiritual as physical—took a couple of years. One of the very first things we did was to take an accounting—a measure of our ecological footprint. We had always thought of ourselves as environmentally aware—using cloth diapers, recycling, never driving a car with more than a four cylinder engine. But when we actually calculated our total use of resources, we found ourselves exactly average for Americans: not bad for a physician's family—since in general the more income people have, the more resources they consume. Yet, we were clearly using more than our fair share on a global scale: six times more energy than our neighbors around the world!

Providentially, as we embarked on our environmental journey, we also began a faith journey. It seemed—at least to us—that the two were inseparable. Coming from two different faith backgrounds, Matthew and I began reading a range of sacred texts—including Hindu, Buddhist, and Hebrew. We listened to the Ramayana on tape together, read parts of the Book of Mormon, and even worked through the beginning of the Koran—but still we did not seem to find any satisfactory answers.

One slow night in the hospital, Matthew picked up an orange Gideon's Bible in the waiting room. He read through one of the Gospels. A light came on. Here were the answers we had been seeking.

Matthew brought the Bible home. One by one, each of us became believers—first Matthew, then Clark, then me, and finally Emma. And that changed everything. Suddenly, the whole family was working off the same page. We had a clear purpose: to love God with all our heart, mind, soul, and strength, and to love our neighbors as ourselves. One way that we could show love for the Creator, and for our global neighbors, was to start taking better care of the planet.

To learn what the Bible had to say about earth stewardship, Matthew read through the entire Old and New Testaments, underlining in orange pencil everything that had to do with nature, creation, and how we are instructed to care for the earth. We found that Matthew 7:3-5 seemed to speak directly to our family: "And why worry about a speck in your friend's eye when you have a log in your own? How can you think of saying to your friend, 'Let me help you get rid of that speck in your eye,' when you can't see past the log in your own eye? Hypocrite! First get rid of the log in your own eye; then you will see well enough to deal with the speck in your friend's eye."

We took Jesus' advice and began cleaning up our own act

before worrying about cleaning up the rest of the world. Over the next couple of years, we downsized our lifestyle, giving away half of our possessions and moving to a house the size of our old garage. Contrary to my earlier fears, we found that the more we "gave up" in material things, the more we gained in family unity, purpose, and joy. Eventually, through many small changes, we reduced our electricity usage and trash production by nine-tenths and our fossil fuel usage by two-thirds.

After we had our own house in order, we felt called to share our journey. Matthew wrote a book called *Serve God, Save the Planet: A Christian's Call to Action.* Using stories from our family's life and the ER, he relayed why we made these changes and inspired others to do the same.

People liked the book—a lot. It's an easy book to read, but hard to ignore. Letters poured in from readers who felt called to change but didn't know where to start. Invitations to speak, preach, and lead workshops came from Washington D.C. to Washington state, from every denomination and faith, from churches with ten members to tens of thousands. People were inspired to change: now they wanted to know how.

In my book, *Go Green, Save Green*, I shared what worked, what didn't, and what we learned in the process. Some steps came easily; others required a new way of thinking or a change of habits. I don't offer a one-size-fits-all plan; each family must decide which changes work best for them, and then keep doing a little bit better every year.

What if someone in your household is not on board? Our daughter Emma, reluctant at first, ended up writing a book for teens called *It's Easy Being Green: One Student's Guide to Serving God and Saving the Planet*, and becoming a leader of the next generation's Christian environmental movement.

Regardless of where you and your family members are on the journey, the book *Go Green, Save Green* provides practical advice on everything from household cleaners, gardening, and fast food—to tips for Christmas shopping, giving away money, and finding quiet time with God.

This is not, however, just a book about practical ways to save time, energy, and money. This is a personal journey of hope. If someone like me can do it, I know you can too! Years ago, back on that island in Florida, two questions—prompted by God—launched our family on this journey.

Today, when making any choice, purchase, or decision, we ask ourselves two new questions: Does this bring me closer to God? And, does this help me love my neighbor?

The answers always lead us down the right path.

# —8—
# Deep Ecology, Or the Spider's Return

## Rev. Alida M. DeCoster

*The Reverend Alida M. DeCoster is currently minister to the Social Justice Internship Program at the Unitarian Universalist Washington DC Office. Ordained in 1986, Reverend DeCoster served Cedar Lane Unitarian Universalist Church in Bethesda, Maryland for twelve years as associate minister. She is also a spiritual director, having completed the Spiritual Guidance Program at Shalem Institute in Bethesda. This sermon was first given at Cedar Lane in 1990. An expanded version appeared in a publication of the UU Ministers' Association. A recent essay, "The Pause That Refreshes: Theological Reflection in Social Justice Ministry," has been published in the collection* A People So Bold *(Skinner House Books, 2009).*

The last time I preached here we were visited by a spider. During the sermon, it crawled all over the pulpit and the microphone. I wonder if it was the same spider that made an appearance last spring when a guest minister was here. That spider crawled all over the preacher! He is braver than I am.

I am sure there are many spiders living in this building. Spiders are loners and they are helpers to humans in that they control the population of insects. Spiders have eight legs and two-part bodies. Insects have six legs and three-part bodies.

I seem to be quite fascinated with these creatures, these "Charlottes" for those of you who loved *Charlotte's Web* by E.B. White. There was one I wrote about in a minister's column some time back who kept building and rebuilding a giant web in the corner of the breezeway by the driveway. It got torn consistently. Now there is always a web in a nearby bush. I guess that spider decided to be more practical. When I came to church on Friday morning, I found our Sexton, Ray, whacking at the ceiling with a broom muttering "Cobwebs . . . cobwebs . . . ." I said, "Ray, I'm writing a sermon about how valuable and wise spiders are!" He replied, "We each have our job to do. You pray for them. I clean up after them."

Fall and Halloween are ripe with mystique. Things are dying in glory all around. Spiders are hard at work. Many species will be laying eggs, depositing them in sacs of silk and dying. This week, I have had many serendipitous experiences with spiders, besides the conversation with Ray. It's almost as if the God of spiders, the Great Arachnid himself, or herself, is aware that I have been working on this sermon.

First, I had breakfast with someone on Tuesday, who, it turns out, minored in entomology in college. She filled me in on some interesting facts about spiders. For instance, did you ever wonder why spiders don't get caught in their own webs? It turns out the spokes of the webs are made of a non-sticky fiber, spider Teflon you might say, and the circular strands are made of sticky material. Notice that the spider always travels on the spokes of the web.

Then, someone else happened to give me a reading from Native American lore on the medicine of spiders, a very helpful piece. But the most amazing thing happened on Wednesday morning. I'd been working for a couple of hours on the first draft of this sermon and was, frankly, feeling frustrated. When I got into my car on that glorious clear morning, there, inside my car, on the passenger's side, connected from window to glove compartment, was a huge, perfect spider web, clinging in the sun. In the middle, perhaps as startled as I, was a large orange spider . . . Inside my car!

Well! Was it a sign? That experience helped me to focus my thoughts and to just use the web itself as an inspiration. I decided to go ahead and drive to church, co-existing with the spider in the car. When I stopped at the stoplights, I would turn to look, somewhat wary, and amazed.

Why are spiders so scary? I asked this of Mary, the former student entomologist. Why are we afraid of spiders? Most are harmless. There are only a couple of dangerous species in North America, and they are rarely, if ever, found around here. Her response was insightful, gleaned more perhaps from life experience than from scientific study of spiders. She thought, and I agreed, that spiders and bugs scare us because they make us feel out of control. They are so sneaky. Nothing seems to stop them. They never appear because we choose to see them, but because they just arrive uninvited. Nonetheless, they are an essential link in the web of life.

When I got to church on Wednesday with my spider companion, I left the window closest to the spider open in hopes that he or she (probably she, as I understand it) would seek more fruitful pastures outside my car. When I came out several hours later, she was still there. Reluctantly I decided that was enough. Gently I opened the door, hoping not to destroy the web. She scurried to the edge of the window where I poked a stick. She climbed on, perhaps ready to move out of that strange contraption, my car. I set the stick down in the leaves. I hope she has a new web. The one in my car finally fell apart by Friday.

At some point in our children's church school education, they are asked to pick which of the Unitarian Universalist Principles is their favorite and tell why. If our children are asked to do that, I suppose the ministers ought to be able to do it. My favorite principle is the one about the interdependent web: We affirm and promote respect for the interdependent web of all existence of which we are a part.

I would like this principle even more if it said we affirm and promote "respect and reverence" for the interdependent web. I'd like to offer some thoughts now on what I associate with the image of the web, both in terms of personal experience and going beyond the human perspective (if that is possible for a human!), to the perspective of the biosphere, all life on earth. I will say a little about the Gaia hypothesis and deep ecology, which is a philosophy combining ecology and spirituality.

The spider web, to our eyes, is an image of connection. There are three kinds of connections that are important in life. We need to feel connected to our own selves, to others, and to Life itself, which may be called God or Higher Power. Connected to self, others and Life. Do you feel connected? Do you feel like you belong in the web of life? What is this journey we are on anyway? The spiritual journey is one of gradual awakening to profound connections. On the journey, we ask these questions, these big "why" questions. We have decided that this is what sets us apart from other creatures. From the point of view of the Gaia hypothesis and deep ecology, however, this very tendency is what makes us so much a part of all that exists and all that happens. You could say that we are the consciousness of the earth. More on that later.

Starting with the personal, do you feel connected? We all feel alone and lonely at times. There is an interesting thing about human development. We have to first develop an ego, a sense of separateness, before we can go beyond it and feel more connected. All developmental theories say this. So we are bound to feel unconnected for at least part of our lives. How can we feel more connected? Is that one reason you come to church? Is it working? What fears are holding you back? We all have fears. We all have limits and we all have needs to feel connected. We need to weave webs of connection, to create relationship. Think of spider webs, how delicate and strong they are, how they are constantly being torn and rebuilt. We need to think of our connections as being both strong and fragile. Here is good medicine—a lesson we can learn from spiders. Don't give up. Life is short. Keep on trying.

Can we weave a web of connection inside our own selves? We often feel disconnected, fragmented, torn. There is too much going on. What is the process by which we learn to forgive and love ourselves? These three, self, other and Life, are all interconnected like the web. We don't come to feel connected in these three ways discretely. They all happen in little ways continuously. If we as individuals decide to say "yes" to Life, if we decide that we are here to grow and create, to build webs, to weave our lives, then we are on the path. Sometimes it is a sticky path and sometimes it is a Teflon path. There are no guarantees. But if we say this fundamental "yes", then connections will begin to happen: connections within, without and beyond.

As for the miracle of Life itself, the more we open ourselves up to awe and wonder and beauty, and see ourselves as *part* of that beauty, part of nature, integral to life, the more we can experience connections and belonging. For many of us, being in nature is a way to do that. Walt Whitman and the Transcendentalists of our own tradition, Emerson and Thoreau, found ongoing revelation of Divine purpose in nature. These are the words of Ralph Waldo Emerson in *The Oversoul*:

> Let us learn the revelation of all nature and thought to our hearts: that the Highest dwells within us, that the sources of nature are in our own minds . . . There is a deep power in which we exist and whose beatitude is accessible to us . . . Within us is the soul of the whole, the wise silence, the universal beauty to which every part and particle is equally related; the eternal One.

Philosophers and poets through time have seen the beauty of the whole and have critiqued an attitude that raises humanity above the plant and animal world to the detriment of all life. We have gotten stuck in our human separateness from nature. St. Francis spoke with the voice of today's eco-justice movement. Ecologist Lynn White, Jr. has written of St. Francis:

> Francis tried to substitute the idea of the equality of all creatures, including humanity, for the idea of humans' limitless rule of creation . . . . The key to an understanding of Francis is his belief in the virtue of humility—not only for the individual but for the human species. Francis tried to depose the human from monarchy over creation and to set up a democracy of all God's creatures . . . I propose Francis as a patron saint for ecologists.

So, what is "deep ecology"? This is a term that was coined in 1973 by Norwegian philosopher Arne Naess. He says that the essence of deep ecology is asking ever more searching questions about human life, society, and nature. "Deep ecology goes beyond a limited piecemeal shallow approach to environmental problems and attempts to articulate a comprehensive religious and philosophical worldview." Respect and reverence for the interdependent web of which we are a part raises some difficult issues about how we live on the Earth. We are in the midst of ecological crisis around the world. To promote the concept of the developing world adopting the consumer patterns that we have enjoyed is to invite global suicide. We must lead the way in living more simply and cooperatively within the limits of our biosphere. The economic and political implications of real interconnectedness cannot be ignored. We have our work cut out for us. Recycling and turning out lights is not enough. We must advocate for sounder environmental policies.

Naess describes the difference between deep ecology and the currently dominant worldview. The dominant worldview still endorses human dominance over nature, sees the natural environment as merely a resource for humans, sees material and economic growth as essential for a growing human population, believes in ample resource reserves, supports high technological progress and promotes consumerism and national centralized communities. The Deep Ecology worldview offers these alternative values: harmony with nature (the nature that we are), the view that all nature has intrinsic worth, biospecies equality, the importance of simplifying material needs, that the supplies and resources of the earth are limited, that appropriate technology should be promoted, that we should do with enough and recycle, that minority traditions should be recognized and local communities strengthened, thereby fostering identity with the biological community in which one lives.

Lovelock and Ellis's "Gaia hypothesis" was first published in the late seventies and has gained fairly wide acceptance in the scientific community. Simply stated, in Lovelock's words, the idea is that "the biosphere is a self-regulating entity, not living, but like a cat's fur, or a bird's feathers, or the paper of a wasp's nest, an extension of a living system designed to maintain a chosen environment . . . Gaia (is) a complex entity involving the Earth's biosphere, atmosphere, oceans and soil: the totality constituting a feedback or cybernetic system which seeks an optimal physical and chemical environment for life on the planet."

We are integral to this system. When we distort this system, other organisms must work overtime to try to retain essential balance for continued life on earth. Lovelock again: "Thus the atmospheric concentration of gases such as oxygen and ammonia is found to be kept at an optimum value from which even small departures could have disastrous consequences for life. The climate and the chemical properties of the Earth now and throughout its history seem always to have been optimal for life . . . For this to have happened by chance is as unlikely as to survive unscathed driving blindfolded through rush hour traffic."

Deep ecological thought makes obvious the need for a major paradigm shift in consciousness. That some humans are sounding the alarm is Gaia in action. I feel like I am just doing my biospheric duty to say that Life itself should be, must be, the central value of human endeavor, not the domination or survival of the human species alone.

The more connected we feel to others and to Life, the more we see the need to change and keep building and rebuilding, weaving and re-weaving. We are not separate, but integral to life on Earth. We have squandered many gifts. Living simply, courageously and in beauty is our challenge. And the medicine of the spider will heal us.

So may it be.

### References

1. Ralph Waldo Emerson, "The Oversoul," from *Singing the Living Tradition*, Unitarian Universalist Association Hymnal (Boston, 1993).
2. Lynn White Jr., "The Historical Roots of Our Ecological Crisis" in *Science*, 1967.
3. Bill Devall and George Sessions, *Deep Ecology: Living As If Nature Mattered* (Salt Lake City: Peregrine Smith Books, 1985), 65.
4. Ibid, 69.
5. J. E. Lovelock, *Gaia: A New Look at Life on Earth* (New York: Oxford Press, 1979, 1987) 11.
6. Ibid 10.

# —9—
# *Global Requiem?*

## Rabbi Stephen S. Pearce, PhD

*Stephen S. Pearce is senior rabbi of Congregation Emanu-El of San Francisco, the oldest Jewish congregation west of the Mississippi River. For twenty years, he was a faculty member in the Human Relations Department of Hebrew Union College-Jewish Institute of Religion in New York City. He earned his PhD in Counselor Psychology from St. John's University. He is a past president of the Northern California Board of Rabbis. He is author of* Flash of Insight: Metaphor and Narrative in Therapy *and co-author with Bishop William E. Swing, the Episcopal Bishop of California and Father John P. Schlegel, President of the University of San Francisco, of* Building Wisdom's House: A Book of Values for Our Time. *In 1997, he established the Interfaith Taskforce to Save the Headwaters Forest, a grassroots effort to save 9700 acres of virgin redwood trees slated to be logged and cut into lumber products. The preserve was acquired by the State of California and the U.S. Government and set aside as a forever wilderness area. The April 2, 2007 issue of* Newsweek *magazine ranked Dr. Pearce as one of the top fifty most influential rabbis in America.*

Ask the beasts, and they will instruct you;
The birds of the sky, they will tell you,
Speak to the earth, it will teach you;
The fish of the sea, they will inform you.

U ntil recently, this admonition from the book of Job (12:7–8)—listen carefully to the messages of earth's creatures—was largely ignored. Now, overwhelming evidence of environmental degradation has propelled ecological issues into the public eye and people are listening, even if they are uncertain what to do. News magazines champion the greening of America, a consciousness further raised by the release of the feature documentary, *An Inconvenient Truth*, an exhaustive catalogue of environmental dislocations, including unusually destructive weather patterns of floods, droughts, hurricanes, and tsunamis. Oil spills; poisoned ground water; global warming —the black tide of climate change; increasingly larger releases of carbon dioxide, methane, nitrous oxide, hydrofluorocarbons and their resultant deterioration of public health; rapidly melting and receding glaciers; rising ocean levels; wildlife and aquatic ecosystem disruptions; over-fished seas; exhausted water resources; spreading deserts; longer temperate seasons in previously never-unfrozen regions; the wanton destruction of millions of acres of rain forests; the reckless harvesting of timber without replacement-planting—leave what may well be an indelible and irreversible mark on the time-line of the twenty-first century. The seemingly insatiable appetite for resources and fuel drives the search for oil in environmentally sensitive areas. Nevertheless, the discovery of new oil and gas resources is not keeping pace with the swiftness at which these resources are being depleted. We are producing mountains of waste that exceed our capacity to recycle and recover resources.

The ever-increasing possibility of drowning in our

own waste was driven home for me by a visit that I made this summer to the ancient Anatolian city of Ephesus (the modern Turkish city of Efes). Originally founded as the Hittite capital city (Apasa or Abasa), by the Roman period, Ephesus was the capital of the western part of Asia Minor, the fourth largest city in the empire. It was an important commercial and export center for Asia, situated at the mouth of the Cayster River on a gulf of the Aegean Sea; it was also the hub of the region's road system. Ephesus featured a theatre capable of holding 25,000 spectators, several major bath complexes, and one of the most advanced aqueduct systems in the ancient world. The enormous ruins reveal a city that by the first century, when Paul (Acts 19:23–41) promoted his new religion there by preaching and writing 1 Corinthians, had grown to at least 250,000 people. However, what I found to be most interesting was not above but beneath the long central market street. Under the paved road ran a huge 2' x 4' sewer system that carried waste downhill into the Aegean harbor. As a result of the waste, the harbor gradually became silted and unusable in spite of repeated dredging. By the Byzantine period, it had become a malarial marsh, forcing residents to abandon the city. Today, the ruins of Ephesus are several miles from the sea. That scene reminded me of an ancient proverb: "Every human being is given the key to the gates of heaven, but that same key also unlocks the gates of hell."

A young man, depressed by evil and suffering in the world complained, "Why did God ever make such a world? Why, I could have made a better world than this myself."

To this complaint he received the terse reply, "That is exactly the reason God put you on this earth—to make it a better place. Now go ahead and do your part."

Like that young man, we, too, have a key that unlocks either of two gates, enabling us to further damage or to repair this already broken world. Whether or not we acknowledge this reality, we seem to be opening the wrong gate. Our planet is dying because we tolerate the despoliation of the earth and sanction abuses that are contrary to our God-given role of stewards of the earth. Everything we do has some environmental consequence, whether intended or unintended. Because fresh air, clean water, natural resources, and plant and animal life seem unlimited, we have taken these precious gifts for granted and have not always been good stewards of the earth.

Jewish tradition teaches that human beings have a noble purpose here on earth, and it is not to allow our virgin forests to be uprooted, our streams and rivers to become contaminated, our wildlife to be deprived of sustenance, and our air to be blackened with the soot of cities and factories.

The Talmud reminds us that Adam, the first human being, was created as a single being to demonstrate that he was a progenitor of successive generations, teaching us that if any creature does not survive, many potential worlds are destroyed. When the last creature of a species dies, it cannot be recreated or replaced. Thus, after the completion of Creation, rabbinic legend asserts that God said to Adam, the first man: "See My world, how beautiful it is. Do not corrupt or destroy it, for if you do, there will be no one to set it right after you" (Koheleth Rabbah 7:13). We are losing species at the extinction rate of one specie every nine minutes. It has been estimated that in 1850, while Darwin was penning his *The Origin of Species*, the rate was one every five years. Historian J.R. McNeill, author of *Something New Under the Sun: An Environmental History of the Twentieth-Century World* (W.W. Norton, 2000), offers this ominous warning: The human species is "playing dice with the planet, without knowing all the rules of the game." His words add urgency to the 1993 statement of the Union of Concerned Scientists, 1670 scientists, including 104 Nobel laureates, who signed the foreboding "World Scientists' Warning to Humanity," a statement that has become all the more urgent today:

> Human beings and the natural world are on a collision course. Human activities inflict harsh and often irreversible damage on the environment and on critical resources. If not checked, many of our current practices put at serious risk the future that we wish for human society and the plant and animal kingdom, and may so alter the living world that it will be unable to sustain life in the manner that we know. Fundamental changes are urgent if we are to avoid the collision our present course will bring about.

Judaism utilizes the Hebrew term *bal taschit* to mean "eco-reverence" from the admonition, *Lo taschit*—"You shall not destroy" (Deuteronomy 20:19). It is a prohibition against waste or wanton destruction of the environment. The author of the book of Leviticus records God's admonition: "The land is Mine and you are my tenants" (25:23). This sober warning against wanton destruction of the environment views creation as an ongoing process in which God and human beings are considered co-partners in safeguarding the earth's riches.

Millennia before oil wells, gas-guzzling SUVs, greenhouse gases, and arithmetically increasing and over-consuming populations, the prophet Isaiah offered this prescient warning: *Lo tohu v'rah-ah lashevet yit-tzee-rah*—"God did not create the world in order that it might become a waste; God formed it for human habitation" (Isaiah 45:18).

Naturally, there are those who hold that the scope of public health, poverty, political and civil unrest, terrorism, and a myriad of other problems dwarf the need to focus on fixing the environment. In addition, some religious leaders view environmentalism as the province of science and fear that such activism can be construed as New Age pantheism and nature worship. Furthermore, an element of our society is trying to discredit the environmental initiatives. For example, in response to *An Inconvenient Truth*, the oil industry-backed Competitive Enterprise Institute has run a series of 60-second spots including one in which an announcer intones, "Carbon dioxide. They call it pollution. We call it life."

Nevertheless, it is important to consider what if anything can be done. Until now, most attempted fixes and attempts to enhance the protection of earth's creatures and natural resources have been five-fold: litigation, legislation, regulation, corporate responsibility, and broad based coalitions of consumer and citizen groups. Each of these approaches must continue to be utilized to strengthen ecological alliances and mandates in order to ensure the survival of earth's diverse species and to protect its resources. However, those efforts seem so overwhelming and unattainable and their impact so remote that they provide those who might like to make a difference with the excuse to say, "What difference can I possibly make?"

Rather than focus on grand plans that seem unachievable, I would like to point out grass root efforts that each of us can embrace by describing our accomplishments at Temple Emanu-El. We have achieved a great deal in a short period of time with a small group of devoted staff members and volunteers.

- In recent months, we signed onto the Congregational Covenant of the California Interfaith Power and Light, promoting responsible stewardship of the planet, raising members' awareness of climate change, and modeling definitive steps to reduce greenhouse gas emissions from Congregation Emanu-El's operations.
- On Eco-Shabbat, held during Earth Day on the weekend of April 22, 2006, among the many activities held was an organized drive to collect outdated computers and small electronics. In so doing, we kept approximately 70,000 pounds of bio-hazardous material out of landfill.
- We have installed clearly labeled recycling bins in all our offices and communal spaces. We are now equipped to recycle paper cups and plates as well as food waste from our many receptions. Our list-serve provides interested members with doable advocacy actions.
- We have completed an energy audit of our buildings and have identified and fixed sources of energy and water waste. We have already implemented numerous energy and water efficient improvements to our buildings including changing 60 watt incandescent light bulbs to 13 or 28 watt compact fluorescent bulbs. Sidewalk and courtyard fixtures have been changed from 150 watts to 35 watts per fixture. All exit signs are now low voltage.
- We have installed automated resource-saving "touchless" bathroom sink fixtures and towel dispensers in two "test" bathrooms where new foam soap dispensers provide a user with 33 percent less soap than previously used.
- We have switched over to green chemical cleaners.
- Bike racks have been installed to encourage carbon dioxide-free trips to the Temple.

- We offer our employees discounted monthly public transit and BART (Bay Area Rapid Transit) passes.
- We offered a free mini-course entitled: "Protect Our Environment—How to Be Part of the Solution," featuring two-hour informational sessions on energy and water conservation, waste reduction, and clean and green cars and homes.
- If every member took just one conservation step, you can imagine the energy, landfill, and water savings that would result. For example, the average home utilizes 2000KW of power per year. By changing over to fluorescent bulbs that typically use 75% less power, the average homeowner can produce significant annual cash savings by eliminating 700KW of electricity. The simple act of disabling your computer's screen saver can save as much as $100 of electricity per year. Multiply those savings by the number of computer owners here today and you can imagine the impact we all can have on the environment.
- Our preschoolers have learned to read the codes on the bottoms of containers in order to help recycle at school and at home.
- Our Pe'ah garden in Colma continues to be the largest provider of organic vegetables to the San Francisco Food Bank. Last year's total of 23,000 pounds of produce were grown by Temple volunteers without the use of pesticides.

Senator Barbara Boxer toured our buildings, spoke at a Shabbat service, and presented the congregation with her prestigious "Conservation Champion Award" in recognition of our efforts to "green" the Temple. At that time, she stated:

> I want you to know how proud and grateful I am for the work that Congregation Emanu-El and California

Interfaith Power and Light are doing together. You are not just keeping California clean and energy efficient, but also are making a difference for our entire planet by your efforts to reduce global warming. Although each of these strategies may seem insignificant, if every citizen were to implement just one effort, you can imagine the environmental impact.

Here are two advocacy things that you can do. In addition to the simple act of changing light bulbs, I encourage you to get involved politically by urging federal officials to promote renewable energy resources, legislate energy star efficiency for all new appliances, provide incentives for the production and purchase of more fuel-efficient automobiles, and follow California's lead in placing a cap on greenhouse gases.

There are many grand statements that I could draw upon to conclude my remarks. After all, care of the earth is not a new mandate for the Jewish tradition as reflected in the admonition of the Torah:

The land must not be sold beyond reclaim, for the land is Mine; you are but strangers resident with Me. Throughout the land that you hold, you must provide for the redemption of the land (Leviticus 25:8–19).

However, I have chosen to complete my remarks with a disarmingly engaging childlike metaphor that points out that this is no longer a problem of some future generation. It is our problem, impacting our lives and those of our children and grandchildren.

The Lorax, Dr. Seuss' mythical character, lives in a

bucolic setting that is being threatened by the overly ambitious and enterprising Once-ler who harvests all the Truffula Trees to manufacture clothes. Unable to stop the inevitable, the Lorax exits, leaving behind a pile of rocks, all that remains of his decimated world; the word "unless" is written on the top. Once-ler, now living in the boarded-up remains of his once proud empire, says to a child who has surveyed the destruction: "But now, now that you're here,/ the word of the Lorax seems perfectly clear,/ UNLESS someone like you/ cares a whole awful lot,/ Nothing is going to get better./ It's not!"

On Yom Kippur, we are challenged to care by choosing life. It is a choice we must make while there is still time before the irreversible tipping point when earth's ability to heal itself spins out of control into the abyss. You can change your habits and embrace a greener lifestyle if you care a whole awful lot. Something can get better before everything is not. On this day of requesting forgiveness, I ask you to make one simple pledge to save just one watt. Amen!

Please note: The presence of mercury in compact fluorescent (CFL) bulbs does require that they be disposed of properly. They should be left whole, and taken to an appropriate recycling site.

# —10—
# Respect of Nature and Natural Resources

## Dr. Muzammil H. Siddiqi

*Dr. Siddiqi was born in India in 1943. He holds a Ph.D. in Comparative Religion from Harvard University. He was President of the Islamic Society of North America for two terms (1997–2001.) He is an adjunct professor in the Department of Religious Studies at Chapman University. He is a founding member of the Council of 100 of the World Economic Forum based in Switzerland. The Council aims to foster dialogue and better relations between Islam and the West. He received the Humanitarian of the Year Award in 1999 from the National Council of Christians and Jews. In September 2001 on the National Day of Prayer and Remembrance, he was invited by President Bush to lead a Muslim prayer at the Interfaith Prayer Service at the Washington National Cathedral. In September 2006, he was again invited by President Bush to lead an interfaith prayer in New York. In August 2006, as part of a special feature called "The West 100", the* Los Angeles Times *recognized Dr. Siddiqi as one of the top 100 most powerful people in Southern California with the following description: "Siddiqi, whose mosque is among the largest in North America, is the religious leader of thousands of Southern California Muslims at a time when xenophobia is running high…. He has been a leader in driving home the point that Muslims in the U.S. are peace-loving."*

Children of Adam, dress well whenever you are at worship, and eat and drink but do not be wasteful: He does not like the people who are wasteful (Al-A'raf 7:31).

It is He who made you trustees of the earth and raises some of you above others in ranks, to test you through what He has given you. Your Lord is swift in punishment, yet He is most forgiving and merciful (Al-A'raf 7:165).

T he role of human beings is that they are Allah's trustees, stewards and agents on this earth. We are not masters of this earth and its resources. Everything belongs to Allah and He has entrusted these resources so that we use them in the right way. As trustees, we have to fulfill the wishes of our Master. We have no right to do whatever we wish. We are responsible and answerable for all our actions. Allah will question us about how we used or abused His creation.

The Word of God, the Qur'an, tells us that the purpose of human life is to serve Allah, live with each other in peace and harmony, and enjoy Allah's creation in nature with gratitude, care, and responsibility according to the rules laid down by Allah.

Islam holds a very positive view of nature. It calls nature the handiwork of Allah (*sun'allah*, al-Naml 27:99) and speaks often of its beauty, value, and goodness. Nature was and continues to be the arena of God's love and grace. Nature, according to Islam, is not fallen. It has not become bereft of value and there is no dichotomy between nature and divine grace. The Wise Creator has created everything for a purpose. The purposiveness of the universe is highly emphasized in Islam.

> We did not create the heaven and earth and everything in between playing (pointless) games. We created them for a true purpose, but most people do not comprehend (Al-Dukhan 44:38–39).

> So set your face to the religion as a man of pure faith. This is the natural disposition of God upon which he created humankind. There is no altering of God's creation (Al-Rum 30:30).

There are religions that teach worship of nature. In Islam we do not worship nature, but we are told that the nature is "muslim." It submits to Allah and glorifies Allah.

> The seven heavens and the earth and all beings therein glorify Him. There is not a thing to do but celebrate His praise, though you do not understand their praise. Indeed He is most forbearing, most forgiving (Al-Isra' 17:44).

> The thunder repeats His praises and so do the angels with awe . . . To Allah prostrate all those who are in heaven and earth willingly or in spite of themselves and so do their shadows in the mornings and evenings (Al-Ra'd 13:13, 15).

Worship imparts worth and value and so one can say

without any hesitation that these statements are mentioned not only to emphasize Allah's greatness and glory but also to create a sense of respect and reverence for nature among humans. Nature is in harmony with worshipping humans or one can say that nature is our fellow worshipper.

Islam teaches that Allah created the natural world a long time before the creation of human beings. Therefore, natural order does not depend on humans; on the contrary, it is humans who depend on the resources of nature. Our responsibility is then to appreciate and enjoy this beautiful nature in all its variety, not to abuse it, waste it or spoil it. We should be thankful to the Creator who gave us these gifts. As trustees of Allah we have to see that we, our future generations and all other creatures of Allah benefit from these resources.

Water is a source of purity and nourishment and so it has to be kept pure and conserved. Air also has to be kept clean and unpolluted because it is essential for healthy living. Trees and plants should be appreciated and should not be destroyed unnecessarily. We should rather cultivate the land with trees and flowers to make it more beautiful. Fish in the sea and all other water animals and land animals have their rights. They should not be destroyed and should not be killed for sport.

There are basically five points that come across as ethical concerns of Islam in our relation to natural resources and the environment:

1. Enjoy natural resources and be thankful to Allah.
2. Use natural resources but do not commit waste or indulge in extravagance.
3. Improve, but avoid corruption and destruction.
4. Keep in mind other creatures who share this planet with

humans.

5.  Keep in mind all human beings and future generations who also need these resources.

In the world today there is not only violence, aggression, injustice, corruption, and immorality but there are also waste of natural resources and pollution of the environment. The result is that now there are problems of global warming, acid rain, ozone depletion, deforestation, floods, drought, and an epidemic of all kind of cancers and unheard of diseases. We must reform our ways to save us and to save the world.

> Corruption has appeared on land and sea as a result of people's actions and He will make them taste the consequences of some of their own actions so that they may turn back (Al-Rum 30:41).

# —11—
# Historic Global Warming Proceedings in the Minnesota House Chambers January 30, 2007

## Archbishop Emeritus Harry J. Flynn

*Archbishop Emeritus Harry J. Flynn was ordained into the priesthood in 1960. He was ordained as bishop of the Diocese of Lafayette, Louisiana in 1986, and became archbishop of St. Paul and Minneapolis in 1995. He currently serves as chairman of the University of Saint Thomas Board of Trustees, and is on the College of Saint Catherine Board of Trustees. On January 30, 2007, Archbishop Flynn spoke before the Minnesota House Chambers on behalf of the Minnesota Catholic Conference, which represents the Roman Catholic bishops from each of the six Dioceses in Minnesota.*

Global warming is an important issue for the state of Minnesota and the entire human family. As a faith community, we take seriously the threat that global warming presents and seek to participate in the solutions. I am here to ask that, as you develop public policies in this legislative session, you bear in mind the urgency of addressing the moral and human dimensions of climate change.

Care for creation is a key principle of Catholic Social Teaching. Rooted in Scripture, the Catholic tradition asserts that the earth and its goods are gifts from God. They are intended by God for the benefit of everyone. Humankind has a responsibility to care for these goods as stewards, not as mere consumers and users. How we treat the environment is a measure of our stewardship and a sign of our respect for the Creator.

In 2001, the United States Conference of Catholic Bishops did a thorough examination of how stewardship of God's creation provides a lens for addressing the warming of the Earth's atmosphere. We bishops published a statement, called *Global Climate Change: A Plea for Dialogue, Prudence, and the Common Good*. Allow me to share with you some of our reflections.

First, the United States bishops accept the findings of the Intergovernmental Panel on Climate Change: that global climate change is occurring, and is at least partially a result of human behavior. What we already know about global warming demands a response.

Second, our national debate over solutions to global warming needs to move beyond the uses and abuses of science, sixty-second ads, and exaggerated claims. The atmosphere that supports life on Earth is a God-given gift, one that unites us as a human family. We must all strive for a civil and constructive debate that recognizes that our common future of tomorrow requires that we act for the common good today.

Third, global warming demands a response from all levels of government. The Minnesota legislature should be among the leaders in our country, creating momentum for our nation to lead the global effort.

Finally, we cannot forget the poorest members of the

human family, who will bear the greatest hardship of global warming. Scientists predict that global warming will induce a greater incidence of extreme weather and violent storms. As Hurricane Katrina taught us with such fearful clarity, the poor are too easily left behind when weather catastrophes occur. The human family has a moral responsibility to act when the dignity of the poor and vulnerable is placed at risk.

Here in the Archdiocese of St. Paul and Minneapolis, we have taken on a unique faithful response to global warming by convening a "Global Warming Action Team." The team is made of parishioners from throughout the archdiocese. We are addressing global warming through concrete, everyday actions, including changing to energy-efficient light bulbs, using public transportation more often, and conducting energy audits of parish facilities. Such efforts make up an important component of the solution to global warming.

I urge you to enact wise public policies in Minnesota that build upon such efforts, to help to avoid the worst effects of global warming and, hopefully, to begin to reverse the damage that has already been done.

As Pope John Paul II said,

> We cannot interfere in one area of the ecosystem without paying due attention both to the consequences of such interference in other areas and to the well being of future generations.

# —12—
# *Creation Care*

## *Dr. Tony Campolo*

*Dr. Tony Campolo is Professor Emeritus of Sociology at Eastern University in St. Davids, Pennsylvania. He previously served for ten years on the faculty of the University of Pennsylvania. He earned his Ph.D. from Temple University. Founder of the Evangelical Association for the Promotion of Education (EAPE), Dr. Campolo has provided the leadership to create, nurture, and support programs for "at risk" children in cities across North America, and has helped establish schools and universities in several developing countries. Dr. Campolo is a media commentator on religious, social, and political matters, having appeared as a guest on television shows such as* The Colbert Report, Nightline, Crossfire, Politically Incorrect, The Charlie Rose Show, Larry King Live, CNN Dayside, CNN News, and MSNBC News. *He co-hosted his own television series,* Hashing It Out, *on the Odyssey Network, and presently hosts* Across the Pond, *a weekly program on the Premier Christian Radio Network in England. He speaks about 350 different times each year around the world for a wide variety of groups. He is the author of thirty-eight books, including his most recent releases in 2010:* Choose Love Not Power *(Regal),* Connecting Like Jesus *(Jossey-Bass) co-authored with Mary Albert Darling, and* Stories That Feed Your Soul *(Regal). Dr. Campolo is an ordained minister, has served American Baptist Churches in New Jersey and Pennsylvania, and is presently recognized as an associate pastor of the Mount Carmel Baptist Church in West Philadelphia. For more information on Dr. Campolo, see* www.TonyCampolo.org.

*The following essay is a chapter from his book,* Letters to a Young Evangelical (The Art of Mentoring), *published by Basic Books, 2006.* **Copyright© 2008 Tony Campolo. Reprinted by permission of Basic Books, a member of the Perseus Books Group.**

Al Gore, our former vice president, has tried to tell us the truth—that we are destroying our natural habitat in ways that are dangerously threatening to our future. We older folks, however, do not seem especially alarmed as he cites climatologist warnings about global warming and biologist predictions of the consequences for all living creatures of our ongoing pollution of land, sea, and air. The good news is that the younger generation seems more attuned to his message, perhaps because more and more schools are including environmental studies as part of the academic curriculum.

The tragedy of environmental degradation became shockingly clear to me when, more than a decade ago, I stood in the north of Senegal with the chief of a local tribe. We were surveying the impact of an ongoing drought that was then affecting the entire Sahel region of Africa. The chief explained that the drought was killing off the herds of sheep and goats that once had been the primary form of sustenance for his people. He told me about the young men of his tribe who, knowing that there was no future for them as shepherds, were leaving to seek employment in the capital city of Dakar. Then he said, "This is not a drought. The people of my tribe know how to survive droughts. We have done that many times over the years. This is not a drought! The earth is changing!"

Of course he was right. The world is changing, and the changes are the result of human irresponsibility. The rain that usually falls in Senegal comes from clouds that are formed over the jungles of the Amazon in Brazil. Those clouds then move across oceans and deliver rain onto the Sahel region of Africa where that chief and his people lived. But in recent years, the rain forests of Brazil have been destroyed at an incredible rate. Entrepreneurs using chop and burn deforestation techniques are turning the Amazon into grazing land for beef cattle. Every hour, an amount of land equivalent to the size of a football field is being deforested. Consequently, the amount of moisture produced in the Amazon decreases each year. That decline is among the factors responsible for what the chief and I observed that hot afternoon as we stood together on the banks of the parched bed of the Senegal River.

One night, on a flight to Argentina, my plane passed over the Amazon. As I looked out of the airplane window, I was awed. As far as I could see, there were fires burning off the jungle to make way for new grazing land. This destruction is the price we are paying to satisfy the world's exponentially growing hunger for beef. As I stared at the fires, I couldn't get my mind off of that African chief and his conviction that the climate of the earth is changing; I realized that this was part of the reason why. Our beef-eating habits are not only leading to clogged arteries, they are also destroying a way of life for a tribe in faraway Africa.

Whenever I bring up my ecological concerns in Evangelical circles, I am fearful of being greeted with suspicion. Right-wing Evangelicals tend to see environmentalists as alarmists who endanger the economic well-being of the country.

There is an alliance of most Evangelicals with the conservative wing of the Republican Party. I believe that this alliance may be largely responsible for such anti-environmental biases. Evangelicals who see [former] President Bush as one of their own born-again brothers supported his anti-environmentalist policies and his repeated argument that we lack sufficient evidence to prove that global warming is happening.

Political conservatives, for the most part, have some justifiable concerns about the possible economic impact of extensive environmental regulation. They worry that compliance with strict government restrictions on industrial waste and other pollutants will impose a great economic burden on American industry and render it less competitive in the global marketplace.

It was this kind of economic consideration that kept President Bush from signing the Kyoto Treaty. This treaty, which was designed to dramatically reduce emissions of carbon dioxide and other atmospheric pollutants, provided certain exemptions to China for several upcoming years. Our president feared that these exemptions would give China an unfair advantage in producing goods for the world market. This, he believed, would not only hurt American business, but also would be to the detriment of all Americans.

Evangelicals are suspicious of environmentalism for other reasons as well. Many Evangelicals believe that environmentalism is part of a New Age movement. But if the New Age movement has been able to make the issue of the environment their own, it is only because the church has put up no resistance and has failed to make environmentalism an important part of its own agenda.

The responsibility to take care of God's creation is prescribed in Scripture. This is clear. In the Hebrew Bible, we read that God requires us to be stewards of creation. We read in the opening chapters of Genesis that God gives to Adam and Eve the responsibility of caring for their natural habitat. Theologians from John Calvin on have made creation care a part of Christian discipleship. In the New Testament, we read such passages as Romans 8:19–22, wherein those who are imbued with the Holy Spirit are expected to reclaim nature from its spoiled condition. It reads,

> The creation waits in eager expectation for the sons of God to be revealed. For the creation was subjected to frustration, not by its own choice, but by the will of the one who subjected it, in hope that the creation itself will be liberated from its bondage to decay and brought into the glorious freedom of the children of God (NIV).

Too many Evangelicals have evaded their responsibility to the environment for far too long. But there are signs that things are changing for the better. Many of us Red-Letter Christians are making the environment one of our primary concerns. For instance, one of the leaders of our movement, Ron Sider, has founded the Evangelical Environmental Network, an organization that is bringing together Evangelicals who share his commitment to environmentalism. Sider is urging us to adopt simpler, less wasteful, and more environmentally responsible lifestyles. This network of Christians is also lobbying the government to do more to protect our environment against polluters. Evangelicals who take our scriptural mandate seriously should support these initiatives and others like them.

When it comes to caring for creation, we Red-Letter Christians have found special inspiration in the life of St. Francis of Assisi. Francis appreciated the sacredness of nature. His famous *Canticle* captures something of his mystical appreciation of God's creation. It is worth repeating here.

> O most high, almighty, good Lord God, to thee belong praise, glory, honor, and all blessing. Praised be my Lord God with all creatures and especially our brother sun, who brings us the day and who brings us the light; fair is he and shines with a very great splendor: O Lord, he signifies to us Thee.
>
> Praised be my Lord for our sister the moon, and for the stars, which he hath set clear and lovely in the heavens.
>
> Praised be my Lord for our brother the wind, and for the air and cloud, calms and all weather by which Thou upholdest life in all creatures.
>
> Praised be my Lord for our sister water, who is very serviceable unto us and humble and precious and clean.
>
> Praised be my Lord for our brother fire, through which Thou givest us light in the darkness; and he is bright and pleasant and very mighty and strong.
>
> Praised be my Lord for our mother the earth, which doth sustain us and keep us, and bringeth forth diverse fruits and flowers of many colors, and grass.
>
> Praised be my Lord for all those who pardon one another for his love's sake, and who endure weakness and tribulation; blessed are they who peaceably shall endure, for Thou, most Highest, shalt give them a crown.
>
> Praise ye and bless the Lord and give thanks unto him and serve him with great humility.

I know that the mysticism implied in this poem will raise some eyebrows among some of our more conservative friends, but we Red-Letter Christians enthusiastically identify with it.

Francis believed that all creatures were created for the explicit purpose of worshipping God. Hence, the annihilation of any species would diminish the adoration that is God's due. He derived such conviction from Psalm 148, which reads,

> Praise the Lord from the earth, you great sea creatures and all ocean depths, lightning and hail, snow and clouds, stormy winds that do his bidding, you mountains and all hills, fruit trees and all cedars, wild animals and all cattle, small creatures and flying birds, kings of the earth and all nations, you princes and all rulers on earth, young men and maidens, old men and children. Let them praise the name of the Lord, for his name alone is exalted; his splendor is above the earth and the heavens (NIV).

I, personally, am sensitized to the Franciscan perspective on animals each year when my wife and I go whale watching off the shores of Provincetown, Massachusetts. The naturalist on the boat with us talks about the decimation of whales and how they are on the verge of extinction. It is then that I remember that the psalmist declared that whales were created to sing hymns of praise to God. Whales sing! At least, humpback whales do. What's more, they create new songs every year. Silencing their voices of worship by annihilating them is sinful. It might even be considered blasphemous.

I'm encouraged these days, as more and more Evangelicals seem to be recognizing the need to be responsible stewards of

God's creation. Recently, the National Association of Evangelicals, an organization representing most Evangelical Christians, issued a strong statement calling for members to join together in personal and political action to protect the environment. Although some of our prominent spokespersons made noises of opposition, this statement marked a significant shift in a positive direction on this issue.

I must bring up another threat to God's creation, perhaps the gravest threat of all: nuclear proliferation. Right now, in a fearful response to terrorism, we are renewing nuclear-production activities and upgrading nuclear-testing facilities. This only encourages nations such as Iran and North Korea to develop nuclear weapons in response. But the danger posed by those two nations is not as great as the danger posed by terrorists such as Osama bin Laden, who has called it a religious duty to secure and use nuclear weapons to destroy Americans. Given that the materials needed to make nuclear weapons exist all over the world, sometimes secured by nothing more than a few guards and a chain-link fence, it is entirely possible that Al-Qaeda terrorists will carry out his wishes.

We Evangelicals, as a people who have been called by Jesus to be peacemakers, should be concerned about the existence of the nuclear threat. The Christian activist William Sloan Coffin, Jr., rightly said, "Only God has the authority to end all life on the planet; all we have is the power." I agree with Coffin that it is time for us to give up that power.

In 1968, our nation, along with forty-two other nations, signed the Nuclear Non-Proliferation Treaty. As of this writing, 189 nations are parties to the treaty. The signing nations who do not have nuclear weapons have promised to forego developing them provided that the nuclear powers eventually disarm. But instead of honoring our treaty obligations, American and the other nuclear nations have lived by a double standard, assuming the right to deploy nuclear weapons and threatening to do so while forbidding the rest of the world to develop them. It is no wonder that the president of Iran mocks America and tells the rest of the world that, given our failure to live up to the Non-Proliferation Treaty, he has no obligation to stop his country's nuclear-development program.

Most Evangelicals remain indifferent to all of this and support a U.S. military that maintains the nuclear threat. Although Billy Graham has spoken out against nuclear arms, most other prominent Evangelicals support the politics of possessing a nuclear deterrent. I suppose that goes with the recent marriage of Evangelicals and conservative politics.

I hope people of faith will realize the importance of dealing with this matter. It is appalling to me that people who claim to take the Bible seriously fail to act urgently for nuclear disarmament. Those of us who know that Jesus called us to be peacemakers (Matthew 5:9) and warned that those who live by the sword will die by the sword (Matthew 26:52) ought to be at the forefront of the nuclear-disarmament movement. Given what we have learned from Paul—that the weapons of our warfare are not the weapons of this world (2 Corinthians 10:4)—Christians should be setting examples for the rest of the world when it comes to taking the risks that make for peace.

On Armistice Day in 1948, General Omar Nelson Bradley said in a speech,

> We live in a world of nuclear giants and ethical infants, in a world that has achieved brilliance without wisdom, power without conscience. We

have solved the mystery of the atom and forgotten the lessons of the Sermon on the Mount. We know more about war than we know about peace, more about dying than we know about living.

Sadly, what he said is especially true of those in our Evangelical community. I hope you will work to change that.

# —13—
# *Touching the Wounds of the Earth*

## *The Reverend Canon Sally Grover Bingham*

*The Reverend Canon Sally Grover Bingham is founder and president of The Regeneration Project (TRP). TRP is primarily focused on its Interfaith Power and Light (IPL) campaign, a religious response to global warming. The IPL campaign includes a national network of 10,000 congregations with affiliated programs in 38 states. Reverend Bingham has brought widespread recognition to the link between faith and the environment. As one of the first faith leaders to fully recognize global warming as a moral issue, she has mobilized thousands of religious people to put their faith into action through energy stewardship. Based in San Francisco, the Rev. Bingham serves as the Canon for the Environment for the Diocese of California and co-chairs the Diocesan Commission on the Environment. She serves on both the National Board on Environmental Defense and the Environmental Working Group as well as the national advisory board for the Union of Concerned Scientists. The Interfaith Power and Light Campaign and the Reverend Bingham have received numerous awards including the 2007 U.S. EPA Climate Protection Award, the Purpose Prize, the Energy Globe Award, and recognition as a "sacred gift to the planet" by the World Wildlife Fund. Reverend Bingham was named one of the top fifteen green religious leaders by Grist magazine. She is the editor of a book which contains a collection of essays about faith and the environment, Love God, Heal Earth (St.Lynn's Press, 2009).*

Today it is fun to be a priest. I am focused on deepening the connection between religion and the environment for both myself and others. It is about saving what God loves, which is all of life. All life is dependent upon the Creator, in whom we live and move and have our being. If you don't like the word environmental because it sounds too liberal, democratic, or political, then call it something else. Call it creation and our role is stewardship. Call it concern for the legacy we leave for future generations. Call it being mindful of your behavior. Call it "loving others as I have loved you." As Christians, you and I are called to be caretakers of God's creation.

I grew up in the rolling hills south of San Francisco near Stanford University. Horseback riding and playing in the open meadows with wildcats, snakes, coyote, foxes, and eagles to gaze upon taught me through experience that we are part of something far greater than we. I learned that we are dependent upon the land, the air, and clean water for life. All of life is dependent upon those things. I watched the birds eat worms, and the vultures strip carcasses clean. I witnessed calves and fowls being born, chickens laying eggs, and eggs hatching. I saw butterflies and moths fly free from their cocoons. Cats in the barn kept the mice population under control. The mystery of life and death on a farm teaches a young child about our interdependence, our place in what poet Mary Oliver calls "the family of things."

There is almost no place in America like that now: places that we might call pristine, which is defined as "still pure and untouched." When we go hiking in the mountains or into a park to sit under a tree, we see Coke cans or plastic bags. Trash covers our beaches, and lies in the bottom of rivers and streams. I go into the wild for peace, for communion with the Divine, for a reminder of my relationship with God, and for quiet time to be alone. I can't find that anymore. There are snowmobiles racing through our national parks, airplanes and helicopters flying overhead, noise from cars, and worst of all, trash.

I love what environmental writer Bill McKibben says about how nature has changed. "There is no more AWAY," he states. Remember when we could throw things "away"? Everything we discard has to find a place to rest, and our waste often pollutes and destroys whatever place it eventually finds. The seas are starting to spit back our waste. Fish are showing high levels of toxins. In many parts of the country, tap water is undrinkable. We have more days every year when the air quality board tells us to stay inside. Breast milk has been found to be contaminated. Sadly, we are doing this to each other and to ourselves.

I think we have lost our way when it comes to the natural world. In his book, *The Last Child in the Woods: Saving our Children from Nature-Deficit Disorder*, author Richard Louv writes that today's children are increasingly disconnected from the natural world. We are into the second generation of people who quite possibly have not had personal contact with nature. Millions of young people haven't walked alone in the woods or thrown rocks into a creek. In previous generations, we played outside, not in front of the TV. We escaped difficult situations by running to nature, and could use the outdoors for healing and quiet time. Nature inspired us to be creative and use our imaginations. Children today have none of that discovery time. Perhaps there is some correlation between high rates of depression in our society and our alienation from nature. Wendell Berry wrote:

> To live we must daily break the body and shed the blood of creation. When we do this knowingly, lovingly, skillfully and reverently it is a sacrament. When we do it ignorantly, greedily, and destructively it is a desecration. In such a desecration we condemn ourselves to spiritual and moral loneliness and others to want.

How we treat God's creation is, at its core, a spiritual issue because it is about how we directly manifest our love for our neighbor and our love for God. How we treat the planet, our fragile island earth, is a manifestation of our relationship with God and with one another. In the Judeo-Christian tradition, God created all that is and called it "good." This makes all of life, human and non-human, sacred. It makes the sun, the moon and the stars sacred. For Buddhists and other religions that teach interconnectedness, there is an understanding that the mistreatment of others is foolish because in the end you are only harming yourself. We are learning that poisoning the land, air or water is harming our neighbor, insulting to the Creator, and damaging to ourselves.

If you profess to be a spiritual person or say you believe in God, then you are expected to show the way and do what is right for the sake of the common good, not what serves you personally. As people of faith, we are the moral voice of society.

When Thomas expressed doubt about Jesus' resurrection, Jesus appeared to show him the truth.

Though the doors were locked, Jesus came

and stood among them and said, "Peace be with you!" Then he said to Thomas, "Put your finger here; see my hands. Reach out your hand and put it in my side. Stop doubting and believe."

Thomas said to him, "My Lord and my God!"

Then Jesus told him, "Because you have seen me, you have believed; blessed are those who have not seen and yet have believed." (John 20:26–29, NIV)

In the past, I asked my congregation NOT to wait until they had seen evidence of global warming. Today, I don't have to ask them to believe in global warming without proof. We are able to put our fingers in the wounds of the earth. Nineteen of the last twenty years are the warmest on record, with 2005 being the hottest. The year 2009 tied with a cluster of other years (1998, 2002, 2003, 2006, and 2007) for the second warmest year on record, according to NASA. Africans in many countries are dying from starvation due to years of drought. High intensity hurricanes due to warmer ocean temperatures are devastating areas like New Orleans. There was a tornado in New York in August 2007. And sadly, we are witnessing the death of polar bears that are drowning from having to swim so far between ice islands where they hunt. The ice caps and glaciers are melting even faster than the scientists predicted a few years ago.

Some day we will have to reckon with how we treated the gifts of creation. God gave us clean resources on which we could depend for our health and well-being. These gifts include the wetlands that filter the water going from land out to sea. We have filled in some 90 percent of them. Coral reefs act as buffers so coastal areas will not be eroded during storms. We are rapidly destroying these essential ecosystems. The huge and magnificent forests all over the world are being cut down before we even know the medicinal value of what is growing there. When we upset and destroy these gifts from God, we are not being good stewards of the earth. It is as if we are saying that we know how to manage these resources better than God. Isn't that why Adam and Eve got thrown out of Eden?

William Keepen, executive director of the Positive Futures Initiative, asks:

> What is it about the human beings in Western culture that permits us to pursue activities that threaten our very survival? What is it that is so important to us that we are apparently willing to destroy the planet—and ultimately ourselves—to get? Why do we persist in these practices even after we realize their self-defeating futility? What does this tell us about our society and our own nature?

Yes, we are a self-oriented culture. The shift from personal self-interest to corporate self-interest is not a huge one. We have been conditioned to believe that bigger is better and more is better. However, humans also help each other in times of stress and disaster. We see it all the time after hurricanes and earthquakes. As people of faith, we need to be mindful of the fact that our choices affect other people, often in faraway places. The choices we make about the food we eat, the cars we drive, the clothes we wear, the coffee we drink, the electricity we use—can often affect others in profound and adverse ways. Might we begin to live our lives in ways that show our love for God?

My working theology is to lead a life that demonstrates love of creation. In this way, I show my love for God. I drive a small car, have a compost pile in my backyard, walk when I can, reduce purchases of things I don't really need, and conserve both energy and water. What is your working theology? Where in your daily life do you show your love for God?

Why not try showing God your love through living a sustainable lifestyle? Winston Churchill said, "We make a living by what we get; we make a life by what we give." Giving and loving God is what makes us Christians. What good is it to be a Christian if we don't in some way lead lives that reflect our faith? Leading by example is what Jesus called us to do.

> By this all men will know that you are my disciples, if you love one another ( John 13:35, NIV).

There is reason for hope and affirmation that makes this ministry not just challenging, but also fun. Besides the corporations like Dupont and Pacific Gas and Electric showing profits after cutting greenhouse gas emissions, we have Interfaith Power and Light programs in thirty-eight states around the country. These programs offer congregations resources for energy-efficient technologies, help with energy audits, and teach money-saving techniques that also benefit the environment. Congregations all over the country are responding with enthusiasm and vigor. Michigan Interfaith Power and Light started up after a small Catholic church in Wyandotte, Michigan used their small wind turbine and solar panel on the roof to provide electricity and lights, a simple meal for the community, and even met payroll during the blackout in the summer of 2003. Congregations are beginning to lead their communities by the examples they set.

There is more good news on the horizon. A range of new ideas and some influential signs of change are happening. In a recent article ("Death of Environmentalism"), authors Michael Shellenberger and Ted Nordhaus question the status quo by asking why a human-made phenomenon such as global warming—which may kill hundreds of millions of human beings over the next century—should be categorized as strictly "environmental." Why are poverty and war *not* considered environmental problems, when we know all of these issues are interrelated? The authors ask, 'What are the implications of framing global warming as an environmental problem— and handing off the responsibility for dealing with it to the environmentalists?'

A report issued by the Pentagon predicts that abrupt climate change could bring the planet to the edge of anarchy. The threat that climate change poses to global stability vastly eclipses that of terrorism, according to the Pentagon report. Lately, conventional wisdom is shifting to include the environment in discussions about peace and security around the world. I am referring to the presentation of a Nobel Peace Prize to Wangari Maathai in recognition of her work in Africa fighting deforestation. Critics of her award asked, "What does tree planting have to do with peace?" The Nobel Committee responds by pointing out that deforestation, soil erosion, and climate change have adversely affected the condition of life for millions of people, leading to hunger and competition for scarce resources. In the Amazon, Haiti, China, and Africa, these conditions have led to an even wider gap between the rich and the poor, conditions which often precede violent outbreaks between populations and eventually become threats to security.

We have no excuse not to change our ways. We have seen and heard and touched the wounds of the earth. As Christians, we should always be moving toward God, getting closer and closer throughout our journey until we are actually walking with God at our side. Everything changes when that happens. With hearts full of grace and angels to help us, we can change our ways first and then gently persuade others. It is faith that gives us courage to do what we must. It is most likely love that will transform us. If we can learn to love the natural world, we will protect it, and if we love one another, we will want future generations to share in the bounty that we have been fortunate enough to enjoy during our time here.

# —14—
# *Interconnections*

## Dr. Zayn Kassam

*Zayn Kassam is Professor of Religious Studies at Pomona College in Claremont, California. She holds a Ph.D. in Religious Studies from McGill University, with a specialization in Islamic and Indian Philosophy. Her research and teaching interests include Islamic ethics, religion and the environment, gender issues, philosophy, and mysticism. Her recent publications include* Introduction to the World's Major Religions: Islam *(Greenwood Press, 2006), and several essays in books, such as* Terrorism and International Justice: A Collection of Philosophical and Political Reflections *(J. Sterba, ed., Oxford University Press, 2003),* Encyclopedia of Islam and the Muslim World *(MacMillan Reference USA, 2004),* A Communion of Subjects: Animals in Religion, Science and Ethics *(P. Waldau and K. Patton, Eds., Columbia University Press, 2006), and* Religion, Terrorism and Globalization: Nonviolence: A New Agenda *(K.K. Kuriakose, Ed., Nova Science Publishers, 2005). She has two books forthcoming, one an edited volume that deals with Muslim women's activism in various parts of the world, and another book that addresses the ways in which Muslims are dealing with gender and globalization issues.*

I n my attempt to understand 9/11, I found that the issues of democracy in Muslim societies, the forces of economic globalization, and the politics surrounding oil were all interconnected, and this short essay explores some of these connections in order to highlight the importance of acting politically and economically in the interest of slowing environmental degradation. The stakes are high: doing nothing now is expected to contribute increasingly to global warming, and to bring about untold human and animal suffering in the decades ahead, as well as species destruction at an alarming rate.

US Secretary of State Condoleezza Rice made the following comment in her speech at the American University in Cairo in June 2005,

> For sixty years, my country, the United States, pursued stability at the expense of democracy in this region, here in the Middle East, and we achieved neither . . . Throughout the Middle East, the fear of free choices can no longer justify the denial of liberty . . . Now we are taking a different course. We are supporting the democratic aspirations of all people.[1]

Such words suggest that perhaps the lack of democracy in the Middle East is not entirely due to what is perceived as the inability of Islam and Muslims to be democratic. Students of Iranian history know that the democratically elected leader of Iran, Mohammad Mossadeq, was removed from office in 1953 in Operation Ajax, planned and executed by the CIA and the British SIS.[2] Aware that the British government derived more revenue from Anglo-Iranian Oil Company than the Persian government did, Iranians decided in 1951 to nationalize the oil industry, after failed attempts to strike a better deal with the

AIOC for more equitable oil profit-sharing between the British and the Iranians.

Clearly our foreign policy interests are tied to our economic interests. To better understand these complex issues, it is necessary to examine globalization. Joseph E. Stiglitz, winner of the Nobel prize in Economics, who served the White House as a member of the Council of Economic Advisors under President Bill Clinton, and also held a post as chief economist and senior vice-president at the World Bank notes that:

> While I was at the World Bank, I saw firsthand the devastating effect that globalization can have on developing countries, and especially the poor within those countries. I believe that globalization—the removal of barriers to free trade and the closer integration of national economies—can be a force for good and that it has the *potential* to enrich everyone in the world, particularly the poor. But . . . if this is to be the case, the way globalization has been managed, including the international trade agreements that have played such a large role in removing those barriers and the policies that have been imposed on developing countries in the process of globalization, needs to be radically rethought.[3]

Pamela Brubaker, who is a Christian ethicist and works closely with the World Council of Churches, details how in 1944 the Bretton Woods institutions, which are the World Bank and the International Monetary Fund, were set up and the groundwork laid for the General Agreement on Tariffs and Trade, to promote economic growth, stabilize the world's currencies, and globalize the world's economies. To these Bretton Woods institutions, another was added in 1995, the World Trade Organization, which was made responsible for setting and enforcing the rules of trade, and to "hear disputes brought against the national or local laws of any country that another member country considers to be a trade barrier."[4] These institutions adopted the economic policies of neo-liberalism and a free market. Dr. Brubaker explains these economic policies quite succinctly:

> The market is to make major social and political decisions. The state should voluntarily reduce its role in the economy. Corporations are to have complete freedom. Unions are to be restrained and citizens given much less rather than more social protection. [5]

Three policies followed from the adoption of neo-liberalism: deregulation, privatization, and liberalization, that were packaged together with structural adjustment programs and an emphasis on export-led growth as conditions for International Monetary Fund and World Bank loans. Deregulation eliminates the control of the state over economic and financial transactions, allowing the market to function freely. Doing so, according to Adam Smith, the great economist, would allow the forces of supply and demand to regulate production and increase economic prosperity, and thereby lift all boats, that is, raise the fortunes of the rich and the poor alike. Privatization again shifted the control of public enterprises to the private sector, and California provides one example of what can happen when private companies such as Enron are made responsible for the public energy sector. Liberalization means ridding the country of protective tariffs and giving up domestic control over trade and finance, and allowing foreign banks to own key economic institutions such as national banks and taking away any barriers to foreign investment. It should be noted that western countries "pushed poorer countries to eliminate trade barriers, but kept up their own barriers, preventing developing countries from exporting their agricultural products and so depriving them of desperately needed export income."[6] In addition, as Korten notes, "any health, safety, or environmental standard that exceeds international standards set by industry representatives is likely to be considered a trade barrier, unless the offending government can prove that the standard has a valid scientific basis."[7] Countries that resist such policies are simply disciplined through the removal of aid and foreign investment and the refusal to trade with them. In other words, such countries are subjected to economic ostracization. The alternative, to put it somewhat crudely, is economic exploitation of the poorer countries by the richer countries.

What this has meant is that instead of enhancing prosperity and eradicating poverty globally, as the Bretton Woods institutions were meant to do through their systems of loans and their policies on trade, wealth has moved upward to the wealthy, the middle class has been handicapped, and the poor have grown exponentially poorer through dispossession and labor exploitation. These are key environmental justice issues. This holds for countries as well as peoples. A study released in 2006 that is based on incomes for the year 2000 asserts that the richest 1 percent of the 3.7 billion adults in the world owned 40 percent of global wealth; the richest 2 percent owned 51 percent; and the richest 10 percent owned 85 percent of global wealth—and these rich are to be found primarily in the United States, Europe, and high-income Asian countries such as Japan, with a few dotted among the elites of other countries. The bottom half of adults in the world owned barely 1 percent.[8] To put this another way, 3 billion people live on less than two dollars a day, and the GDP of the forty-eight poorest countries is less than the wealth of the three richest people in the world. Furthermore, 51 percent of the world's one hundred wealthiest bodies are corporations.[9]

It is clear that the pursuit of wealth through globalization is a key factor in increasing poverty. In addition, wealth generation is predicated on energy resources to make it happen. We can't transport anything, grow food, have pesticides and fertilizers, continue with industrial production, and meet the needs of our much-too-rapidly expanding world population without energy, and without water. And both are at risk. Thus, another connection comes into view: that western political interests in the oil-bearing regions of the world, which are now joined by China and India's interests in the same, are directly tied to economic growth and the benefits that globalization delivers to industrialized capitalist societies.

The energy needs underlying corporate economic growth explain why the western world, which owns much of the world's wealth, is so keenly interested in the oil-bearing countries, whether Saudi Arabia, Iraq, Iran, Kuwait—the largest producers, or Venezuela, and why there are conflicts in the Sudan even though these conflicts are presented to us in the media as government-sponsored militia groups enacting genocide on what they call non-Arab African Muslims or non-Muslims such as Christians and tribal religious groups. The media rarely mentions the salient factor that Sudan has oil and that the conflicts we see there are largely centered on regions where oil extraction is about to take place or underway.

However, our dependence on oil raises two issues of

extreme concern. First of all, the American scientist Hubbert predicted that global oil supplies would peak in about 1995 or 2000,[10] which it would have, had the oil embargo of the 1970s not extended that for a few more years. Although many scientists predict oil extraction will peak anytime between now and 2020, some analysts such as the noted Princeton geologist Kenneth Deffeyes have declared that the peak is already upon us.[11] What this means is that while there is still lots of oil in the ground, henceforth it will be extracted in increasingly diminishing quantities and at greater costs of production. Although oil will continue to be extracted in 2025, the world's population, which is expected to be around 8 billion at that time,[12] will further stress the need for energy. As China and India, two countries that have benefited immensely from globalization, join the industrialized world, they too will add to the demand for energy to fuel their economic growth and as they increase their consumption of energy utilizing goods such as cars and refrigerators, associated with a prosperous western lifestyle. What this means is that globally, we need to be thinking very seriously about alternate energy sources. The documentary film *How Cuba Survived Oil* provides an eye-opening account of the distress caused to a society when access to oil is severely reduced as it was after the dismantling of the Soviet Union and the oil embargo imposed on it, and the steps that need to be taken in order to address the food and energy needs of the nation.

The other facet is the impact using fossil fuels such as oil has on our environment. Carbon emissions are a key contributor to global warming and hence to a rapidly deteriorating environment, as are greenhouse gases such as methane. Huge quantities of methane are produced by the meat industry alone, not counting the amounts being released into the atmosphere as our Arctic ice shelves melt. In addition, the destruction of carbon sinks, those natural bodies such as forests that absorb carbon from the earth's atmosphere, in the search for profits reduces the earth's capacity to naturally correct for the greenhouse gases being thrown into the earth's atmosphere through human activity. In addition to the clearing of vast tracts in the Amazon for the livestock industry, Indonesia's forests are being cleared at an alarming rate in order to establish palm oil tree plantations, a cash crop. This destruction is funded by foreign and local corporations who themselves are aided by governments interested in following the Bretton Woods institutions' policies in diverting countries from sustainable agriculture to cash crop agriculture in order to export such crops to industrialized countries where they can be converted to products sold at a much higher price. Palm oil is used in so many processed foods and products that it has become a necessary ingredient and hence a lucrative industry. But the price being paid—sending 2 billion tons of greenhouse gases into the atmosphere annually as valuable forests are destroyed—is one that creates short-term gain and profit for a few. It does this while pushing so many off their lands, forcing laborers to work long hours for little pay, destroying their health, especially women's health as a result of the aggressive pesticides that are used, which are themselves oil-based, and the effluents from palm-oil production also destroy waterways and coral reefs. Ultimately what this shortsighted focus on profit does is that in the name of globalization, wealth creation, and supposedly lifting all boats, this fragile and beautiful planet that is our only home is at risk of dying with untold suffering along the way. Books such as *God's Last Offer*, by Ed Ayres,

Michael Klare's *Blood and Oil*, or any of David Korten's books, among many others, lay out the environmental challenges that lie before us and the economic connections to be made with environmental justice issues and environmental degradation. It is now a well-known truism that environmental degradation is accompanied by concomitant exploitation of humans and other animals.

Many have seen Al Gore's documentary, *An Inconvenient Truth*. Some may think this documentary is simply a device to introduce mass hysteria and that really, there is nothing to worry about because the earth always heals herself. But people of faith, surprisingly, across religious traditions, but certainly in this country, are sitting up and taking notice. They are asking: did not God say you have dominion over the earth? Yes. But did God say destroy the earth? Perhaps stewardship of the earth was what God meant? One Christian leader in this country who has come under fire but shown tremendous foresight and courage, is Richard Cizik, the former vice president of governmental affairs for the U.S. National Association of Evangelicals. He has called upon evangelical Christians to "return to being people known for our love and care of the earth and our fellow human beings." He preaches the doctrine of creation care, which is a Bible-based understanding of why Christians have a duty to be environmental stewards. Pope Benedict XVI recently stated, "The world is not something indifferent, raw material to be utilized simply as we see fit. Rather, it is part of God's good plan." He has called for protecting the Amazon, and has recently denounced factory farming.[13] All over the globe people of faith are calling for better stewardship of the earth, regardless of their religious tradition, whether the Dalai Lama,[14] or the Aga Khan. Ironically, Native Americans, the very peoples who have suffered so much in our desire for their land, have always told us that all of creation is interconnected and all its constituents are in relationship with one another, and are interdependent.

These are times that call for a war on the deleterious inequalities being introduced by globalization's excesses, and these are times that call for a renewed commitment to the sustainability of our planet, without which our pursuit of freedom, democracy, dignity, and peaceful coexistence will be meaningless. Indeed, as the planet suffers, resource wars will reach unimaginable levels, including wars over water—one can live without oil, but not without water. If, as Gandhi said, one should become the change one wishes to see in the world, then the time to act is now. A first step would be to rethink the current processes through which economic growth is facilitated, even worshipped, at a cost that unquestionably is too high to bear.

**Notes**

1. http://news.bbc.co.uk/2/hi/middle_east/4109902.stm.
2. http://www.iranonline.com/NewsRoom/Archive/Mossadeq/.
3. Joseph E. Stiglitz, *Globalization and Its Discontents* (New York: WW Norton & Co., 2003, 2002), ix-x.
4. David C. Korten, "The Failures of Bretton woods" in Richard C. Foltz, ed., *Worldviews, Religion, and the Environment* (Belmont, CA: Wadsworth/Thompson, 2003), 567.
5. Pamela K. Brubaker, *Globalization at What Price? Economic Change and Daily Life* (Cleveland: The Pilgrim Press, 2001), 27.
6. Stiglitz, 6.
7. Korten, 567.
8. www.wider.unu.edu/.../2006-2007-1/wider-wdhw-launch-5–12-2006/.
9. http://www.globalissues.org/TradeRelated/Facts.asp.

10. http://www.lifeaftertheoilcrash.net/.

11. http://www.princeton.edu/hubbert/current-events.html.

12. http://www.populationaction.org/Publications/Reports/ Mapping_the_Future_of_World_Population/Summary.shtml

13. http://www.grist.org/news/maindish/2007/07/24/religious/ index.html.

14. http://hhdl.dharmakara.net/ hhdlspeech.html#environment.

# —15—
# Climate Change:
# A Rabbi Speaks Out

*Rabbi Warren G. Stone*

*Remarks from The Washington Summit*
*on Climate Stabilization,*
*Climate Institute 2007*

*Rabbi Warren Stone has served as rabbi of Temple Emanuel in the Washington metropolitan area since 1988. Rabbi Stone came to the Washington area after serving congregations in California and Texas. He received his B.A. from Brandeis University. He received his M.A.H.L. and Rabbinic Ordination from Hebrew Union College-Jewish Institute of Religion in New York and a D. Min. in Religion and Psychotherapy from Andover Newton Theological School. He received an Honorary Doctorate of Divinity from Hebrew Union College-Jewish Institute of Religion in 2003. Rabbi Stone is known nationally for his leadership on Religion and the Environment. He is the founding chair of the Central Conference of American Rabbis' Committee on the Environment. Rabbi Stone represented many national Jewish organizations as the Jewish United Nations delegate at the UN Conference on Climate Change in Kyoto, Japan in 1997, and again in 2009 in Copenhagen, Denmark, where he blew the Shofar and led a number of interfaith programs and prayer vigils. He also serves as co-chair of the National Religion Coalition on Creation Care and on the International Advisory Board for Earth Day International. He has led delegations on environmental issues to the Congress and White House. Rabbi Stone was honored with opening a session of the U.S. Congress in 1998. In 2002, he co-*

*chaired a Senate conference with Senator Joseph Lieberman and members of the native Gwinchin people calling for protection of the Arctic National Wildlife Refuge. He has spoken several times at rallies at the U.S. Capitol on environmental issues. He has received a distinguished merit award from the National Conference of Christians and Jews and a Merit award for his work on Judaism and the Environment from Shomre Adamah of Washington, D.C. Rabbi Stone has had articles published in* The Washington Jewish Week, Reform Judaism Magazine, *and* Central Conference of American Rabbis Journal. *His article, "A Jewish Response to Climate Change", was published in The Climate Institute's book,* Sudden and Disruptive Climate Change. *His abstract, "Climate Change Beyond Diplomacy: Thinking Outside the Box", was presented at the International Congress of Scientists in Copenhagen and served as a paper for the UN Conference on Climate Change in Copenhagen, Denmark 2009.*

An ancient Jewish midrash teaches that when God took Adam around the Garden of Eden and showed him its magnificence and splendor, God spoke to him saying, "If you destroy it, there is no one else besides you!"

Those words ring mightily today, for the very future of life as we know it is at stake. I fervently believe that climate change, with the destruction that it is wreaking on our fragile, sacred earth, has become the most profound religious issue of our times. Like Adam, we have been warned and cannot plead ignorance; like Adam, will we fail to heed God's words?

Who is responsible for responding to the challenge of global climate change? We tend to think that it is the scientist, the statesman, and the environmentalist upon whom this responsibility lies. But climate change is an urgent moral and spiritual issue for all peoples of our world. We are witnessing its impact right now, and we can foresee the havoc it will wreak on the health and survival of further generations. The future will bring environmental refugees in numbers unknown in previous ages. As a result of climate change and habitat destruction, a myriad of species now faces a silent genocide.

As a rabbi and religious leader, I am concerned about our common future, the quality of life for our families, and the threatened species of our world, including our own. I join fellow religious leaders in that concern. But it is not enough to care about climate change, forest devastation and environmental threats to clean water, air, and seas. It is incumbent upon every religious leader, religious institution, and person of faith to serve as beacons to our communities, illustrating by our actions and example our spiritual commitment to our earth and its threatened and limited resources.

In a world where matters of faith seem so often and so tragically to divide us, there is no issue that aligns us more deeply than our shared dependence upon and sacred responsibility to this tiny planet, enfolded within its fragile atmosphere, spinning in the vastness of time and space. I experienced this shared conviction most profoundly when, in 1997, I served as the Jewish NGO representative at the United Nations climate talks in Kyoto, Japan. I met with Catholic, Protestant, Muslim, Hindu, and Buddhist leaders from around the world. We spoke at Kyoto's largest Buddhist Temple, and all concurred that our human actions, our sins, have damaged the environment. Each speaking from the voice of his or her own authentic spiritual tradition, we affirmed our religious responsibility to act. Amidst Buddhist chanting, I blew the shofar, a ram's horn, the blast of sound that has been Judaism's ancient call to action since the days we wandered, searching for our way in the desert.

I carried this profound experience back to my own

country and my own community. Here, too, I found that faith traditions can readily unite on issues of climate change. Working for many years with the National Partnership on Religion and the Environment, I have joined interfaith leaders to lobby on Capitol Hill and to meet with White House staff. Political leaders are eager to hear our religious point of view. Statements by Catholic bishops, Protestants leaders, rabbis and tribal leaders have symbolic power and carry political weight. Formal resolutions affirmed by hundreds of thousands of persons of faith help embolden our legislators to act. In 2007, religious leaders stood with sympathetic legislators on the U.S. Capitol's steps, raising our voices to stop the drilling in the Arctic National Wildlife Refuge. The opportunity to be heard is greater than in previous decades, and we have a prophetic responsibility to seize it. Bold initiatives are needed—and needed now—to protect species, to create incentives for the development of alternative energies, to protect endangered coastal areas, and to mitigate our dependence on fossil fuels.

Of course, our collective, interfaith efforts gather their strength from the work each of us does within our own particular communities. As chair of the Environmental Committee of the Central Conference of American Rabbis, I have joined with many committed colleagues to use our faith tradition to increase awareness and encourage action in response to climate change and other environmental challenges. We have passed national resolutions on climate change and energy policy and have established environmentally conscious guidelines for our myriad congregations around the country. For example, we recently celebrated Chanukah, the Jewish holiday of light, renewal and commemoration of bold action that honors one's faith. During the holiday, we mounted a very successful COEJL (Coalition on the Environment and Jewish Life) national campaign—"Let There Be (Renewable) Light! or How Many Jews Does it Take to Change a Light Bulb?" Thousands of congregations encouraged their members to install CFL bulbs in their synagogues and homes and to add to their holiday ritual a ceremony that calls this generation to environmental action, in response to the moral imperatives of our own times.

And finally, I believe that our religious voice must be strongest closest to home, manifest in how we daily live. The congregation I serve, Temple Emanuel of the Greater Washington D.C. area, has worked on greening its agenda for eighteen years. We believe that local action by religious communities can have a national and international impact. The congregation I serve has installed solar panels on the roof for our eternal light, added wind power from a regional collective, made use of energy efficient zoning, lighting, and office equipment and in our building phase made use of passive solar throughout the building. We planted a sustainable garden to meet our annual ritual needs, growing grapes, horseradish, and indoor olive and pomegranate trees. We regularly schedule environmental Shabbats and other opportunities for learning with our state representative and national leaders. We sell CFL bulbs and have information about climate change on our coffee tables. We have become an EPA energy star community and one of the nation's first "zero carbon footprint" communities by supporting Carbonfund.org and their alternative energy investments. Our web page www.templeemanuelmd.org includes our Green Shalom Action Guide which is designed to educate and spur further community involvement and environmental action in our own homes and community. This community focus has borne fruit, with a good number of our young people choosing science, media, religion, and public policy arenas that deal directly with environmental issues.

There is so much that each of us can and must do, within our own homes, congregations, and communities, and beyond, as we work together, in common cause, to preserve and sanctify life. Religious communities have a crucial moral role in affirming the profound need to engage on the issue of climate change.

As Rabbi Tarphon of the second century reminds us: "It is not your duty to finish all the work, but neither are you at liberty to desist from it." May it be that years hence, our children and our children's children will look back with appreciation to this moment when we heeded one of the great moral imperatives of our time. May they know that we had the vision and the strength to fulfill our sacred obligation to preserve and protect the earth in all of its majesty, this garden with which we have been entrusted, for those who will follow.

# —16—
# *Walk Humbly*

## *The Reverend Dr. Ignacio Castuera*

*Ignacio Castuera holds a Doctor of Religion degree from the Claremont School of Theology. He was the first Mexican-American district superintendent of the United Methodist Church serving in the Los Angeles District. He went on to become the pastor of Hollywood United Methodist Church for eleven years, where he transformed the church into a center of the growing movement aimed at creating a positive religious response to the AIDS pandemic. An accomplished preacher and author, Dr. Castuera edited a collection of sermons gleaned from those given on the Sunday after the infamous L.A. riots. The book,* Dreams on Fire: Embers of Hope: From the Pulpits of Los Angeles After the Riots, *became one of the top ten religious books of 1992. In November 2004, he was the Jameson Jones Preacher in the Prophetic Tradition at the Iliff School of Theology. He is the first national chaplain for Planned Parenthood of America, and currently serves as the senior pastor of Trinity United Methodist Church in Pomona, California.*

With what shall I come before the Lord and bow myself before God on high? Shall I come before him with burnt offerings, with calves a year old? Will the Lord be pleased with thousands of rams, with ten thousands of rivers of oil? Shall I give my first-born for my transgressions, the fruit of my body for the sin of my soul?

God has shown you, O human one, what is good. And what does the Lord require of you, but to do justice, and to love mercy, and to walk humbly with your God? (Micah 6:6–8)

T he book of the Prophet Micah has been the source of many great sermons, hymns and even of the quotation that is on the pedestal of the statue that the now extinct Soviet Union gave to the United Nations in New York: *And they shall beat their swords into plowshares and their spears into pruning hooks.*

I would like to indicate that Micah's message is also most relevant for people of faith wishing to address the ecological crisis from a religious perspective. This book is shared by the Abrahamic religions: Judaism, Christianity, and Islam. If these three religions were to take seriously the way in which this book can address the problems of pollution and systematic destruction of our ecosystem, we would have the potential for change unmatched by any other organization.

When one reads the whole book of Micah, and it is not a very long book, the thing that is striking is the way in which the author connects injustice to people with effects upon the earth. A few samples should suffice to demonstrate the way these concerns are brought together by the prophet:

For behold, the Lord is coming forth out of his place, and will come forth out of his place, and will come down and tread upon the high places of the earth. And the mountains will melt under him and the valleys will be cleft, like wax before the fire, like waters poured down

a steep place. All this is for the transgression of Jacob
and for the sins of the House of Israel (Micah 2:1).

It does not take much imagination to see in this text
a hint of the effects of global warming upon the earth. But it
is important to read ahead and understand the nature of the
*transgression* and *sins* that Micah has in mind. These sins and
transgressions have to do primarily with social and economic
inequalities. Micah understands the connection between
those who cut trees and those who undercut the poor and
dispossessed. Ecological degradation is highly correlated with
economic discrepancies and this is why the prophet writes:

Woe to those who devise wickedness and work
evil upon their beds! [This is not a reference to
sexual sins, read on!] When morning dawns they
perform it, because it is in the power of their hand.
They covet fields, and seize them; and houses,
and take them away; they oppress a man in his
house, a man and his inheritance (Micah 2:2).

Micah means that during the night, when people rest
upon their beds, the evil ones think of ways to deprive the
powerless of the few possessions they have. The whole book
has variations on these twin themes of the degradation of
people and of the environment.

Precisely because of this central theme of Micah's
message it is imperative that the often-quoted verse at the
top of this sermon be seen with a different lens, now that the
ecological degradation he foresees is truly upon us. The cure
for the sickness that the prophet diagnoses is in this beautiful

message: *do justice, love mercy, and walk humbly with God.* Here are just a few brief comments about the first two parts of the formula that Micah gives before concentrating on the third part of the solution:

## Do Justice

There is confusion in the Western world when one deals with legal language. This springs from the fact that two types of law have influenced the cultures and languages of the Western Civilizations: Judaic and Roman law. If we used either *Torah* or *lex* when we used the word law, the problem would be reduced. The same happens with the word "justice." The biblical word for justice is *tzedakah* and it can be translated as "justice" or "righteousness" but it is also translated many times as charity, adding to the confusion. When people say they want to bring a criminal to "justice," they usually mean that they want the full weight of the law (*lex*) to fall upon the outlaw. But when theologians talk about justice for the oppressed we mean "equity" and "restoration" instead of legal revenge.

When Micah states that God wants people to "do justice" he means work so that the injustices he has pointed out in his book are undone. Restoration and restitution are essential for the fulfillment of the vision of instruments of war being converted into implements of agriculture (swords into plowshares).

## Love Mercy

Mercy has a variety of meanings ranging from personal charity to clemency. Unfortunately, charity is the way in which this term is understood most of the time. Of course charity is important, but only as a way of practicing compassion on a daily basis in preparation for the clemency that must be exercised when the role reversal envisioned by the prophet occurs. The best way to explain this is by referring to the work of the Truth and Reconciliation Commission in South Africa.

The daily works of charity done by both whites and blacks during the days of apartheid prepared them to grant clemency to the perpetrators of injustices committed during the grim days of forced separation of the races. It is not accidental that a Christian, Bishop Desmond Tutu, was influential in the creation of the Truth and Reconciliation Commission. He was a man of mercy during the tough days of apartheid and then, when blacks came into power and Nelson Mandela became the first black president of the new South Africa, Tutu was in a position to advocate for "mercy" as clemency. The book *No Future without Forgiveness* is a compendium of Bishop Tutu's penchant for mercy as forgiveness and clemency.

## Walk Humbly with Your God

The last part of Micah's formula for pleasing God is the one that has been paid less attention over the centuries and yet it is the one that is most important and relevant for our days of global warming and potential ecological catastrophe. Walking with God is a concept that in and of itself has power to change our behavior. It implies that the person who "walks with God" is trying constantly to consult the Divine presence as decisions are faced. However, it is the term *humbly* that bears close attention.

"Humbly" obviously is an adverb that conditions our "walk with God." The adverb is related to the noun "humility" which is often misunderstood because it is severed from its etymology, its origin. The origin of the word "humility" is in the Latin term "humus," the earth, the soil, the clay out of which, as Genesis says, humanity is created. "Humanity," in fact, is also related to the word "humus" as is, strangely enough, "humor." The biblical equivalent is "adama" from which the name of the first human, Adam, comes. (This is only in one of the sources in Genesis; in the alternate story in Genesis 1, "Ish" and "Isha" are created at the same time and there is no creation out of Adam's rib!) This is important because it is established from the beginning that humanity is interrelated, and interdependent with the earth. Humility means to act in accordance with the awareness of the fact that people are part of the whole web of life and that the best response to that awareness is to "tend" the earth, not to dominate and subdue all the parts of this veritable paradise called Earth.

Walk humbly with your God today must mean, be aware of your "carbon footprint" much more than any other track you might leave in the "sands of time." Carbon footprint is a very important term for people of faith to learn and teach so we can leave a sustainable earth for our descendants. One easy way to understand this concept is to remember that all the energy humans use produces a certain amount of carbon dioxide, and the higher the use of energy, the larger the carbon footprint. Walking humbly with our God today must mean using less and less energy and leaving much smaller carbon footprints to minimize our stress on the environment.

Walking humbly with our God must translate into specific actions and efforts, some easy and some most inconvenient. Walking and bicycling must replace use of the automobile for short trips. Combining errands and car pooling must be adopted when using a motorized vehicle of any kind. Use of public transportation must be increased thereby improving the income of those companies and contributing to much more efficient service.

Water usage at home can be drastically reduced if gardens are converted to native grasses and plants. Drinking water from our own faucets instead of buying bottled water will dramatically decrease the use of hydrocarbons to make the water bottles. Many articles and editorials have been appearing across the United States praising potable water and encouraging people to return to the efficient and inexpensive ways of drinking water. Showers should be shortened and water should be turned off while scrubbing.

Food consumption should concentrate on products grown as close to the consumer as possible. Here again several great experiments have been documented and published. The New York Times had a story about a family that lived a whole year on food grown locally. Bill McKibben, author of many books defending the environment, has done the same and published the experience in his book *Deep Economy*.

Legislative efforts must be started or supported at all governmental levels to improve the conditions that would make it easier to accomplish the humble walking with God that Micah believes is the true sacrifice acceptable to God.

Recently some people in industrialized societies in an effort to make up for their larger carbon footprint have started to "pay" for their excessive use of carbon dioxide by making contributions to ecological efforts to protect the earth. This is a sad, even if well intentioned, attempt at making up for abuses of the environment and it creates a gulf between those who can pay extra for their energy use and those who cannot. A more desirable proposal would be to require carbon dioxide emission producers, those who make the most money by selling hydrocarbons, to pay heavily without necessarily passing on the cost to the consumer. An ecology tax for those who produce and consume the most products with carbon dioxide emissions is not only desirable, it is urgent.

## A Most Important Postscript

The text quoted above starts with four questions asking what should a person do to please God. Even a casual reading ought to convey the scathing critique that Micah levels against the Temple establishment. The questions escalate in a crescendo of ridicule starting with what appears to be a simple and honest question and moving towards ridiculous exaggerations. It is amazing that what was intended as an attack against the priestly authority of Israel can today be seen as a most severe warning.

Harkening back to the story of Abraham's attempted sacrifice of Isaac, the prophet asks: *Shall I give my first-born for my transgressions, the fruit of my body for the sin of my soul?* Today God would answer:

> You are giving not only your first born, but all your progeny, to the god of consumerism! You are mortgaging your children's future and the future of all creation with your blindness, your desire for more and more profits, more and more convenience, more and more and more. Then God would add, I already told Micah and the people of ancient Israel what they must do: to do justice, love mercy, and to walk humbly with your God. WALK HUMBLY WITH YOUR GOD!

# —17—
# Sustainable Development in Islam

## Dr. Safei-Eldin Hamed

*Safei-Eldin Hamed is a scholar of environmental planning and international development. He received his Bachelor of Architecture from Cairo University, his Master of Landscape Architecture from the University of Georgia, and his Ph.D. in Environmental Planning from Virginia Tech. He has taught at various universities in Canada and the USA and is currently Director of Landscape Design Programs at Chatham University. From 1994–1996, he worked as an "environmental assessment specialist" at the World Bank in Washington D.C. Dr. Hamed has authored five books, among which is* Landscape Planning Objectives for the Arid Middle East: An Approach to Setting Environmental Objectives *(Edwin Mellen Press, 2002). He also co-authored seven books and wrote more than sixty chapters, articles, papers, and special reports in the areas of environmentally and socially sustainable tourism development, and environmental strategies and policies for developing arid lands and coastal deserts. His research bridges theory and practice, architecture and landscape architecture, development and conservation, North America and the Middle East, and science and culture.*

In 1987, the World Commission on Environment and Development, commonly known as the Brundtland Commission, published a report titled, "Our Common Future" and coined for the first time the term "sustainable development." Gradually, the term was brought into common use and led to unprecedented political consensus regarding today's global environmental challenges. It also triggered a worldwide debate among environmentalists who struggled to define precisely what sustainable development is and why is it important to achieve it.

This essay discusses the above questions, and then focuses on the relationship of the concept of sustainable development to Islam, both as a popular, widespread ideology and as a body of knowledge that provided its followers throughout their history with a distinct system of environmental ethics and comprehensive criteria of decision making.

## The Significance of Achieving Worldwide Sustainable Development

The 20th century was primarily associated with three global phenomena that affected the environment, namely: urbanization, industrialization, and population explosion. The need for sustainability arose from recognizing that the destructive, extravagant, and inequitable nature of these trends, when projected into the future, leads to biophysical impossibilities. An assessment of the global environment reveals the following principles and trends.

- The Earth's physical and life systems are governed by nature's laws.
- The Earth's life system is dependent on its physical conditions.
- Humans have changed the quality of the physical

environment, and are striving to sustain that quality.

- Humans, as a part of the Earth's life system, are completely dependent on the system.
- Humans have used science and technology to exploit physical and life system resources.
- The human economic system does not ensure that nonrenewable resources are kept accessible in the future. Rather, it encourages excesses and wastefulness, and fails to account for depreciation of natural capital.
- On the whole, humans have contributed very little towards the well being of Earth's life system.

## Defining Sustainable Development

The Brundtland Commission defined sustainable development as:

The development that meets the needs of the present generation without compromising the needs of future generations.

Other scholars advanced that concept and generally agreed that sustainable development aims at four major objectives:

- *Fulfilling the basic human needs of the society, i.e., food, water, shelter, and air,*
- *Protecting the natural systems that support life,*
- *Attaining inter- and intra-generational equity, and*
- *Reconciling the often competing objectives of economic prosperity, environmental integrity, and social equity.*

## Achieving Sustainable Development Objectives in Islam

- *Fulfilling the basic human needs*

A Muslim believes that he is put on earth as God's steward, and that God is the ultimate owner of the earth. As a trustee of Allah (God), humankind has to contribute to the task of *isti'mar al-ard* (the development of the earth).

> Then We appointed you stewards in the earth after them, to see how you would behave (Qur'an 10:15).

An ultimate objective of the *Shari'ah* (Islamic law) is the universal common good of all created beings. The Prophet Muhammad declared that all creatures are the dependents of Allah, and must serve Him by filling their ordained roles, so as to best benefit each other" (Mishkat, Vol. 2, 613). He also encouraged Muslims to plant and conserve trees, keep and treat kindly domesticated animals, and avoid all types of pollution as asserted in his most ecologically significant saying: "Cleanliness is half of the faith."

- *Protecting the natural systems that support life*

Muslims believe that all known and unknown creatures in the universe are valuable, and that each performs a dual function: a social function in the service of humankind and a spiritual function as an evidence of the Creator (Ba Kadr, 15). Natural systems that support life are addressed in the Holy Qur'an and the Sunnah (The Prophet's Tradition). Water, for example, as the origin of life is mentioned in several chapters of the Qur'an stressing its multiple uses:

> We made from water every living thing (Qur'an 21:30).

> It is He who has made the sea subject, that ye may eat thereof flesh that is fresh and tender (Qur'an 16:14).

> And he caused rain to descend on you from heaven to clean you therewith (Qur'an 8:11).

A primary goal emphasized in *Shari'ah* is the conservation of water and other vital ecosystems that are necessary for the preservation and continuation of life. Recognizing that these are indispensable for the life of all creatures, Islam made their use the privilege of all people, without discrimination, monopoly, or corruption.

> And tell them that the water is to be divided between them (Qur'an 54:28).

Also, most scholars interpret Prophet Muhammad's saying: "People are partners in three things: water, pasture and fire," as an injunction for each society to share vital resources like water, land and energy. A similar emphasis is found in the Qur'an and Hadith regarding air, flora, fauna, and other earth resources.

The Qur'an, for example, highlights the vital functions that air performs including the ones that humans knew like sailing and moving clouds.

Behold! In the creation of the heavens and the earth, in the alteration of the Night and Day, in the sailing of the ship through the Ocean for the profit of humankind (Qur'an 2:164).

It also mentions other functions that human knowledge was lacking at the time of the Qur'anic revelation, namely pollination.

And we send the fecundating winds (Qur'an 15:22).

A close companion of the Prophet summed up the Islamic attitude toward life: "Act in this world as if you will live eternally, and act for the hereafter as if you will die tomorrow."

- *Attaining inter- and intra-generational equity*

Sustainable development implies sustainable levels of production and consumption. However, if current levels of production and consumption continue, future generations will likely be more in numbers and poorer in standards of living than today's generations. Certainly, this situation is neither just nor equitable to one's offspring.

Islam considers justice and equity as one of the most fundamental elements of its value system (Ati, 36). The Qur'an urges Muslims to be just with all creatures including whom they differ from or don't know. Future generations and other nations who share the same planet in time and space fall under this injunction.

O you who believe! Stand out firmly for justice,

as witness to Allah, even as against yourselves,
or your parents or your kin (Qur'an 4:135).

The juristic rule stating, "What leads to the forbidden is itself forbidden," indicates that any human activity that unfairly harms others or mars the vital functions of their natural systems is a sin and thus unlawful under Islamic law.

Do no mischief on the earth after it has
been so well ordered (Qur'an 7:56).

Islam also cares about the preservation of all species and their genetic qualities. Prophet Muhammad advised his followers to avoid marrying their close relatives to ensure a stronger and healthier offspring. In brief, an equitable inter- and intra-generational relation depends on maintaining the ecological balance of the entire Cosmos.

And the earth We have spread out, set thereon
mountains firm and immovable; and produced therein
all kinds of things in due balance (Qur'an 15:19).

- *Reconciling the often competing objectives of economic prosperity, environmental integrity and social equity*

Despite the emphasis of the *Shari'ah* on the issues of society, family, and life, the ultimate value in Islam is neither material nor economic, but moral. To establish the Kingdom of Allah on earth is the mission of each devout Muslim, but the eternal bliss in the hereafter is the essence of Islam (Manzoor, 160). Under this encompassing paradigm, the arbitration between differing interest groups is made easier within an Islamic State where decisions are based on a three dimensional typology that assigns priorities to different human objectives. Absolute necessities such as human life, offspring and family, mental health, and private property have the highest priority. Lesser wants such as safety and security follow, and last are refinements and perfections such as aesthetics and recreation (Ibn Taimiyya, 1966).

This criteria is illustrated in the works of Abu Ishaq al-Shatbi, a prominent Muslim jurist of the thirteenth century. Based on *Shari'ah*, he developed a remarkable method of environmental assessment that helped him decide whether a certain project should be carried out or not. Al-Shatbi made his decisions by weighing social benefits against costs through the investigation of eight issues:

1.  Is the impact of the injury general, or does it affect only a small group of people?
2.  Is the injurious effect certain to occur, or is it only slightly probable?
3.  Is it large and substantial, or small and negligible?
4.  Is the injury intended by the individual, being a part of the motive behind his project?
5.  If the individual does not intend to inflict injury, is he aware or not that his action may cause injury?
6.  Is the injury accompanied by some general good? If so, is that general good itself very important so that it must be achieved; or can it easily be forgone?
7.  What is the importance of the project's gain to the individual's own economy? Can he stand its loss, or not?
8.  Are there alternatives to achieve the same end, which

involve no injury, or lesser injury, compared with the initial project? (Siddiqi, 1972)

## Ideas for the Future

Sustainability of the earth is vital for the future well-being of humanity. This can only be attained by having an ordered universe based on solidarity of purpose and a commitment to ethics and values. Islam could play a major role in this venture, particularly since it has been for sometime a rich, yet untapped source of environmental ideas, ethics, and ideals.

# —18—

# *Chaos or Community*

## *The Reverend Dr. Bob Edgar*

*Dr. Bob Edgar is president of Common Cause. He is an ordained elder in the United Methodist Church, former General Secretary of the National Council of Churches, and a former president of the Claremont School of Theology (1990 – 2000). Dr. Edgar is well known for his service as a six-term member of the U.S. House of Representatives, where he served on the Select Committee on Assassinations (1976–78) that investigated the deaths of Dr. Martin Luther King, Jr., and President John F. Kennedy. His wide-ranging career has also included pastorates at United Methodist congregations, and stints as a teacher, college chaplain, community organizer, and director of a think tank on national security issues. He received his B.A. from Lycoming College, and a Master of Divinity from the Theological School of Drew University. He holds four honorary doctoral degrees. Dr. Edgar serves on the boards of the National Coalition for Health Care, Common Cause, the National Religious Partnership for the Environment, and the Environmental and Energy Study Institute. He has garnered awards from the American Legion, Vietnam Veterans of America, and the National Taxpayers Union.*

**(The following sermon was delivered by The Reverend Dr. Bob Edgar in Nebraska 2006.)**

May God bless us with discomfort at easy answers, half-truths and superficial relationships, so that we may live deep within our hearts.

May God bless us with anger at injustice, oppression, and exploitation of people, so that we may work for justice, freedom and peace.

May God bless us with tears to shed for those who suffer from pain, rejection, starvation, and war, so that we may reach out our hands to comfort them and turn their pain into joy.

And may God bless us with enough foolishness to think that we can make a difference in this world, so that we can do what others claim cannot be done (Franciscan Benediction).

Hello, my name is Bob and I am a recovering energy addict and consumer addict.

I want you to let your mind go back a long way (for some of you before you were born) to February 1968—I was all of twenty-two years of age and I was a senior at theological school. I was invited by this Bill Coffin guy who was the chaplain at Yale and later became the preacher at The Riverside Church in New York. I was invited to Washington DC for the very first time to talk about the issues of poverty and peace.

February 1968, I accepted the invitation and I got on a bus. We went down to Washington to The New York Avenue Presbyterian Church and as we were getting off the bus, the face of the radical religious right wing community of the day—a guy by the name of Carl McIntyre—was holding up a great big sign. It read, "Kill a Commie for Christ's sake." I crossed the picket line and entered the church and went up into the balcony and speaker after speaker spoke about poverty. The keynote speaker was a young clergy person, age 39; the Rev. Dr. Martin

Luther King, Jr.

Five weeks later, Dr. King was assassinated. Less than ten years later, as a young member of Congress, I served as one of the twelve members of the Select Committee on Assassination looking into Dr. King's death. I am fortunate to be one of the few people who have interviewed James Earl Ray at Brushy Mountain State Penitentiary as well as having met Dr. King.

But more importantly, I want to share some words of Dr. King's that are relevant to this discussion about global warming. In a book called, *Where Do We Go from Here: Chaos or Community*, listen to what Dr. King says: "We are now faced with the fact, my friends, that tomorrow is today. We are confronted with the fierce urgency of now. In this unfolding conundrum of life and history, there is such a thing as being too late. Procrastination is still the thief of time—life often leaves us standing bare, naked, and dejected with a lost opportunity. The tide in the affairs of humanity does not remain at flood—it ebbs. We may cry out desperately for time to pause in her passage, but time is deaf to every plea and rushes on. Over the bleached bones and jumbled residue of numerous civilizations are written the pathetic words 'too late.'"

He closes that statement by saying that we still have a choice today—"nonviolent coexistence or violent co-annihilation."

This may well be humankind's chance to choose between "chaos and community." The reason I share that quote with you is this. As a person of faith whose [former] organization is made up of thirty-five different and differing denominations that separately represent about 45 million constituents in 100,000 congregations, and works closely with the U.S. Conference of Catholic Bishops, with the Islamic Society of North America, with the Jewish community and other faith traditions who represent people from across the board—people from the right, the left, and the middle theologically—I know that tomorrow is today and we must act together.

I believe that the life issue of our time is global warming. I believe that God is calling us to pay attention on this issue. I can find no place in scripture whether Christian, Jewish, Muslim, or other where God is calling us to participate in the destruction of the planet. Every place I look God is calling us to be stewards of the earth—He puts us in a garden that we mess up. But now God is calling us to this moment.

> We are the leaders we have been waiting for.
> We are the leaders we have been waiting for.

That's my first point. I have served in Congress. I have met various presidents from Jimmy Carter, Bill Clinton, George H. W. Bush and George W. Bush. I have met the egos of our members of Congress, most of whom are very nice, but we cannot wait for our political leadership to be the leaders we have been waiting for, especially on the issues of climate change and global warming, peace and justice. We are the leaders that we have been waiting for.

We have this unusual thought that if we could just convince enough of the political leaders to move, we can make a difference. But I believe to really energize our nation we have to energize ourselves and take back our leadership role. Dr. King did not become the leader of the civil rights movement by going to college or going to seminary to take on that role. He simply had that attitude of being courageous in the midst of great civil violence—he stood up when other people told him to sit down and spoke up when others told him to be silent.

We are the leaders we've been waiting for, and in this dark time, our eyes have to be opened and seeing more clearly. In this particular time in history, we need to act. I met with Tony Blair, the [former] prime minister of England when he brought twelve religious leaders to the British embassy in August 2005. He wanted to talk to the president, but he also wanted to meet with some religious leaders. He invited some of the religious right to the meeting. He brought the Roman Catholics to the meeting. He brought some of the Southern Baptists to the meeting and he brought some moderate to progressive leaders. We talked about global warming because it is one of his passions and at the end, he turned to those who agreed with the technology and the science and he said you know the urgency of now, you know we must act, you know we are getting close to the tipping point. And then he turned to my colleagues on the far religious right and he said for those of you who don't believe the science, who question whether we should act now, you have to act now too in case you are wrong because by the time you get it, it may be too late.

We are the leaders we've been waiting for.

My second point is that we have to understand the state of the world in which we are living. I want to sum this up really quickly. The world has been in existence for about five billion years and human life has been on the planet for who knows how long. However, we discovered oil in 1830, a year the population reached one billion. We reached two billion people 100 years later in January of 1930. Then thirty years later when I was in high school we reached three billion people. Fifteen years later when I was elected to the U.S. Congress there were four billion of us. I served six terms, twelve years and then in 1987 when

I left congress there were five billion of us on the planet and come October 15, 1999 we reached six billion. [Currently there are about 6.8 billion of us.]

The first statistic I want to share is, in the last 100 years 95 percent of everything created by human hands has been recreated. The second statistic I want to share with you is more than half of all the people who have ever lived on planet earth are alive today wanting access to energy. If China and India were to have a lifestyle like the west has had over the last fifty years, whatever you pick, whether you are conservative and say we have 500 years of oil left, or others who say we have seventy-five years of oil left, the bottom line is our rate of consumption of dwindling resources. There is no doubt that globally, our resources are being utilized at ever increasing rates, and our reserves of oil, gas and water will not last forever.

We are the leaders we have been waiting for and we better act quickly, as people of faith from a variety of faith traditions know that God is calling us to understand the nature of both our nation and our world.

This brings me to my final point. As leaders, as people who know we have a responsibility as the faith community to act, I am part of something called the National Religious Partnership for the Environment. I got folks to laugh awhile back with the "What Would Jesus Drive?" campaign.

Our evangelical brothers and sisters, I and a few folks from the Reform Jewish tradition did a funny thing on November 20, 2002. We flew to Detroit and were picked up by Roman Catholic nuns driving a hybrid electric-gasoline car. Rabbi David Saperstein hopped in the front and evangelist Ron Sider of Evangelicals for Social Responsibility and I sat in the back and the nun is driving a Prius automobile as we head to

William Clay Ford's office. On the side of the car it says, "What Would Jesus Drive?" and the rabbi's hand is tapping on the word "Jesus" as we head off.

We sat down with Bill Ford. And we went to speak with the autoworkers at General Motors. At that time, no U.S. car company was making hybrids and they were spending thirteen billion dollars telling all of us that we wanted to buy SUVs. We put pressure particularly on the Ford Motor Company and the moral pressure that we had as people of faith to change their 'be-attitude' and I am proud to say that a couple of years later Ford came out with the Ford Escape, a hybrid automobile—it isn't enough, but it's a beginning.

We are the leaders that we've been waiting for to call each other to task and our churches, our synagogues and our mosques—the group that I call middle church—not the far right or the far left, but the people in the middle must take ownership for the world in which we live.

One of my favorite theologians is Lily Tomlin. She was cast in a play called *A Search for Intelligent Life in the Universe*. Her character in this one-actor play is Trudy the bag lady. She is a homeless woman who dresses in rags, carries all her belongings in two bags, and has a hat with an umbrella on it because no one mugs a lady with a hat with an umbrella on it.

She stands at the corner of Walk and Don't Walk Streets as the play opens, waiting for aliens from outer space. She has been hired by those aliens to search for intelligent life in the universe and the entire play is her gathering information she keeps on little yellow post-its all over her body. Specifically, I want to share the ending with you.

One of the aliens comes up to Trudy and says to her, "Trudy, before we go back into outer space we need one more

piece of information—can you tell us about the goose bumps?"
Trudy replies, "You have come from outer space and you want
to know about goose bumps?" And then it dawns on her that
the last time she had goose bumps she was at a Broadway play.
She takes the aliens to a Broadway play and they stand in the
back watching. About two-thirds of the way through the play,
she looks down and they are covered with goose bumps—and
then she discovers they weren't watching the play at all. They
were watching the people.

The final scene is Trudy outside looking up into the dark
sky and she says, "I come out here every night and I look up into
the sky and I know they are watching us and I see the funny
things we do to each other and I hear them laughing. But most
nights I look up and I know they are watching our inhumanity
to each other; our destruction of the planet; our violation of
human rights and civil rights and children's rights and people's
rights; our destruction of the environment; and I hear them
crying."

My hope is that you, as the leaders that we have been
waiting for, will help to give the universe goose bumps by
taking seriously this life issue and joining with others in all
faith traditions and some in non-faith traditions and give the
whole world goose bumps.

Maybe some day you and I will do something so
wonderful for this planet that it will give the whole universe
goose bumps.

# Index

# D

# E

# M

# Q

# S

# Y

Yale 21, 170

Yellowstone 8

yoga 62

Yom Kippur 102

# Z

Zen 62